Windows® 7

maranGraphics™

COURSE TECHNOLOGY
CENGAGE Learning™

Australia • Brazil • Japan • Korea • Mexico • Singapore • Spain • United Kingdom • United States

Trademarks

maranGraphics is a trademark of maranGraphics Inc. Maran Illustrated, the Maran Illustrated logos and any trade dress related to or associated with the contents or cover of this book are trademarks of maranGraphics Inc. and may not be used without written permission.

The Course Technology PTR, Cengage Learning logo is a trademark of Cengage Learning and may not be used without written permission.

Windows is a registered trademark of Microsoft Corporation in the United States and/or other countries.

All other trademarks are the property of their respective owners.

All images © Cengage Learning unless otherwise noted.

Important

maranGraphics and Course Technology PTR, Cengage Learning have attempted throughout this book to distinguish proprietary trademarks by following the capitalization style used by the source. However, we cannot attest to the accuracy of the style, and the use of a word or term in this book is not intended to affect the validity of any trademark.

Copies

Educational facilities, companies, and organizations located in the U.S. and Canada that are interested in multiple copies of this book should contact Course Technology PTR, Cengage Learning for quantity discount information. Training manuals, CD-ROMs, and portions of this book are also available individually or can be tailored for specific needs.

COURSE TECHNOLOGY
CENGAGE Learning™

Course Technology™, a part of Cengage Learning
20 Channel Center Street ■ Boston, MA 02210 ■ http://www.courseptr.com

maranGraphics is a family-run business.

At **maranGraphics**, we believe in producing great books—one book at a time.

Each maranGraphics book uses the award-winning communication process that we have been developing over the last 30 years. Using this process, we organize screen shots, text and illustrations in a way that makes it easy for you to learn new concepts and tasks.

We spend hours deciding the best way to perform each task, so you don't have to! Our clear, easy-to-follow screen shots and instructions walk you through each task from beginning to end.

We want to thank you for purchasing what we feel are the best books money can buy. We hope you enjoy using this book as much as we enjoyed creating it!

Sincerely,

The Maran Family

We would love to hear from you! Send your comments and feedback about our books to family@maran.com

To sign up for sneak peeks and news about our upcoming books, send an e-mail to newbooks@maran.com

Please visit us on the Web at:

www.maran.com

CREDITS

Author:
Ruth Maran

Technical Consultant:
Robert Maran

Project Editor:
Kim Benbow

Technical Editor:
Lisa Bucki

Layout Design & Illustrations:
Jill Flores
Mike Tanamachi

Indexer:
Larry Sweazy

Proofreader:
Heather Urschel

**Publisher and General Manager,
Course Technology PTR:**
Stacy L. Hiquet

**Associate Director of Marketing,
Course Technology PTR:**
Sarah Panella

**Manager of Editorial Services,
Course Technology PTR:**
Heather Talbot

ACKNOWLEDGMENTS

Many thanks to the talented team that was involved in the creation of this book.
I would especially like to thank Megan Belanger, Kim Benbow and Jill Flores for
their enthusiasm, hard work and dedication. Thanks also to Lisa Bucki and
Heather Urschel for their diligent reviews.

Finally, to Richard Maran who originated the easy-to-use graphic
format of this guide. Thank you for your inspiration and guidance.

TABLE OF CONTENTS

Chapter 1

WINDOWS BASICS

Chapter 2

FUN AND USEFUL PROGRAMS

Chapter 3

Chapter 4

TABLE OF CONTENTS

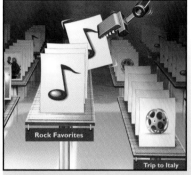

Chapter 8

SHARE YOUR COMPUTER

Chapter 9

BROWSE THE WEB

TABLE OF CONTENTS

Chapter 10

EXCHANGE E-MAIL

Chapter 11

EXCHANGE INSTANT MESSAGES

Chapter 12

WORK ON A NETWORK

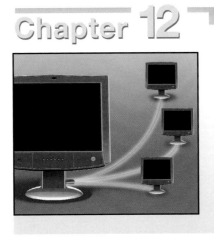

Chapter 13

OPTIMIZE COMPUTER PERFORMANCE

Windows Basics

INTRODUCTION TO WINDOWS

Microsoft® Windows 7 is an operating system that controls the overall activity of your computer.

Windows 7 is available in several different editions. The Windows 7 edition installed on your computer determines the programs and features available to you.

WINDOWS 7 EDITIONS

Windows 7 Home Premium

The Windows 7 Home Premium edition is the recommended choice for home users.

Windows 7 Professional

The Windows 7 Professional edition is the recommended choice for small business users and for people who work at home where security and productivity are essential.

Windows 7 Starter

The Windows 7 Starter edition offers basic Windows 7 functionality and will come pre-installed on some small, inexpensive laptop computers called netbooks.

Windows 7 Ultimate

The Windows 7 Ultimate edition is designed for computer enthusiasts who want all the programs and features that Windows 7 offers.

Windows 7 Enterprise

The Windows 7 Enterprise edition is designed for large companies and organizations.

WINDOWS 7 FEATURES

Work with Files

Windows helps you manage the files stored on your computer. You can open, print, delete, move and search for files. You can also create new folders to help you organize your files.

Share Your Computer

If you share your computer with other people, you can create user accounts to keep the personal files and settings for each person separate. You can assign a password to each user account and easily share files with other users.

Work with Photos, Music and Videos

Windows allows you to copy photos from a digital camera to your computer and print your photos. You can also play music CDs on your computer while you work and create playlists of your favorite songs. You can also play videos and create DVDs using your favorite home movies.

Work on a Network

Windows allows you to share information and printers with other people on a network. You can set up and access a wired network as well as a wireless network, which allows computers to communicate without using cables.

Customize and Optimize Windows

Windows offers many ways that you can customize your computer to suit your preferences. For example, you can change the desktop background and change the sounds your computer makes. You can also use the many tools that Windows provides to optimize your computer's performance.

Access the Internet

Windows allows you to search the web for information of interest, keep a list of your favorite webpages and quickly return to webpages you have recently viewed. You can also browse the web privately without leaving any trace of your web activity.

USING THE START MENU

You can use the Start menu to start programs, open files, change computer settings, get help with Windows and more.

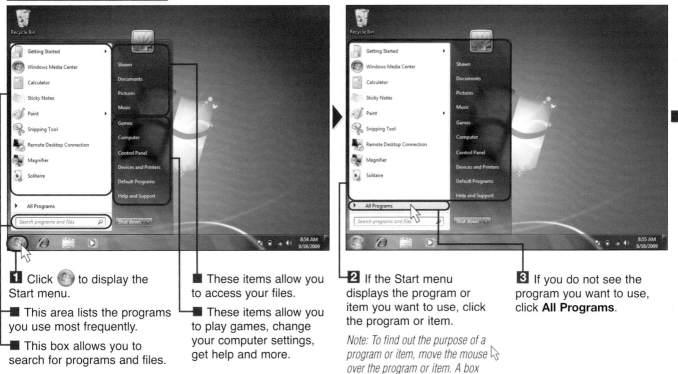

The programs available on the Start menu depend on the software installed on your computer.

USING THE START MENU

1 Click 🟦 to display the Start menu.

■ This area lists the programs you use most frequently.

■ This box allows you to search for programs and files.

■ These items allow you to access your files.

■ These items allow you to play games, change your computer settings, get help and more.

2 If the Start menu displays the program or item you want to use, click the program or item.

Note: To find out the purpose of a program or item, move the mouse over the program or item. A box appears, displaying a description of the program or item.

3 If you do not see the program you want to use, click **All Programs**.

Tip

Which programs does Windows provide?

Windows comes with many useful programs. Here are some examples.

Calculator	Sticky Notes
Display a calculator on your screen.	Create sticky notes that appear on your screen.
Desktop Gadget Gallery	**Windows DVD Maker**
Add gadgets to your desktop, such as a clock or weather gadget.	Make DVDs that include photos and videos from your computer.
Disk Cleanup	**Windows Media Player**
Remove unnecessary files from your computer.	Play music, videos, CDs and DVDs.
Internet Explorer	**WordPad**
Browse through information on the web.	Create and edit documents.

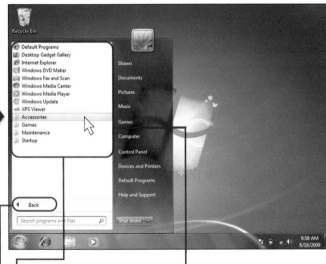

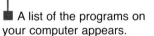

■ A list of the programs on your computer appears.

■ If you want to once again display the programs that appeared when you first opened the Start menu, click **Back**.

4 Click the program you want to use, or click a folder (📁) to display its contents.

Note: To close the Start menu without selecting a program, click outside the menu.

■ If you selected a folder in step **4**, a list of the programs in the folder appears.

5 Click the program you want to use.

Note: You may need to click another folder (📁) before you can see the program you want to use.

■ The program opens. In this example, the Calculator program opens.

6 When you finish working with a program, click ✖ to close the program.

SCROLL THROUGH A WINDOW

You can use a scroll bar to browse through the information in a window. Scrolling is useful when a window is not large enough to display all the information it contains.

If your mouse has a wheel, you can use the wheel to scroll through a window. To scroll down, roll the wheel toward you. To scroll up, roll the wheel away from you.

SCROLL THROUGH A WINDOW

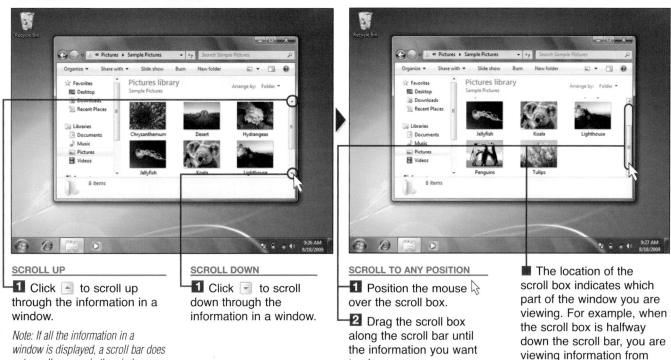

SCROLL UP

1 Click ▲ to scroll up through the information in a window.

Note: If all the information in a window is displayed, a scroll bar does not usually appear in the window.

SCROLL DOWN

1 Click ▼ to scroll down through the information in a window.

SCROLL TO ANY POSITION

1 Position the mouse ▱ over the scroll box.

2 Drag the scroll box along the scroll bar until the information you want to view appears.

■ The location of the scroll box indicates which part of the window you are viewing. For example, when the scroll box is halfway down the scroll bar, you are viewing information from the middle of the window.

CLOSE A WINDOW

When you finish
working with a
window, you can
close the window
to remove it from
your screen.

CLOSE A WINDOW

1 Click 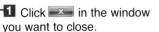 in the window
you want to close.

■ The window disappears
from your screen.

*Note: If you close a document
without saving your changes, a
message will appear, allowing
you to save your changes.*

If a window covers items on your screen, you can move the window to a different location.

You may also want to move windows so you can see the contents of multiple windows at once.

1 Position the mouse over the title bar of the window you want to move.

2 Drag the mouse to where you want to place the window.

■ The window moves to the new location.

You can easily change the size of a window displayed on your screen.

Increasing the size of a window allows you to view more information in the window. Decreasing the size of a window allows you to view items covered by the window.

RESIZE A WINDOW

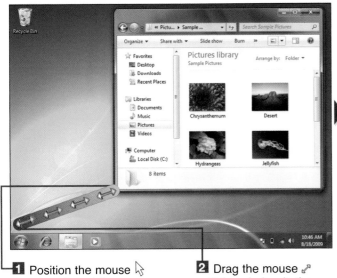

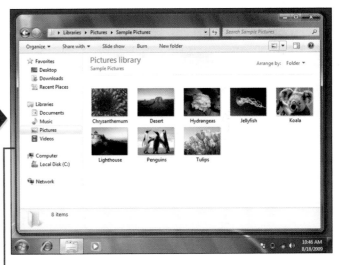

1 Position the mouse ⌖ over an edge of the window you want to resize (⌖ changes to ↗, ↘, ↔ or ↕).

2 Drag the mouse ↗ until the window is the size you want.

■ The window displays the new size.

Note: You cannot resize a maximized window. For information on maximizing a window, see page 22.

MAXIMIZE A WINDOW

You can maximize a window to fill your entire screen. This allows you to view more of the window's contents.

MAXIMIZE A WINDOW

1 Double-click the title bar of the window you want to maximize.

■ You can also click ▣ in a window to maximize the window.

■ The window fills your entire screen.

■ To return the window to its previous size, double-click the title bar of the window.

■ You can also click ▣ in a window to return the window to its previous size.

22

MINIMIZE A WINDOW

If you are not using a window, you can minimize the window to temporarily remove it from your screen. You can redisplay the window at any time.

Minimizing a window allows you to temporarily put a window aside so you can work on other tasks.

MINIMIZE A WINDOW

1 Click ▬ in the window you want to minimize.

■ The window disappears from your screen.

■ To redisplay the window, click the icon for the window on the taskbar.

Note: If you have more than one window open in the same program, a preview of each open window will appear. Click the preview of the window you want to redisplay. For more information, see page 26.

MINIMIZE ALL BUT ONE WINDOW

If you have several windows open but only want to focus on one window, you can instantly minimize all the other open windows on your screen.

MINIMIZE ALL BUT ONE WINDOW

1 Position the mouse over the title bar of the window you want to focus on.

2 Press and hold down the mouse button and shake the window on your screen. Then release the mouse button.

■ Windows instantly minimizes all the other open windows on your screen except the window you chose to focus on.

■ To once again display all of your open windows, repeat steps **1** and **2**.

SHOW THE DESKTOP

You can temporarily hide all the open windows on your screen so you can clearly view your desktop.

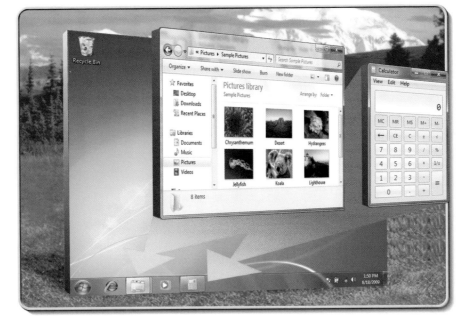

SHOW THE DESKTOP

OPTION 1

1 To instantly make all the open windows on your screen transparent, position the mouse over the box at the bottom-right corner of your screen.

■ Windows makes all your open windows transparent so you can clearly view your desktop.

■ To once again display all your open windows, move the mouse away from the bottom of your screen.

OPTION 2

1 To instantly minimize all the open windows on your screen, click the box at the bottom-right corner of your screen.

■ Windows minimizes all your open windows so you can clearly view your desktop.

■ To once again display all your open windows, click the box again.

SWITCH BETWEEN WINDOWS

If you have more than one window open on your screen, you can easily switch between the windows.

Each window is like a separate piece of paper. Switching between windows is like placing a different piece of paper at the top of the pile.

SWITCH BETWEEN WINDOWS

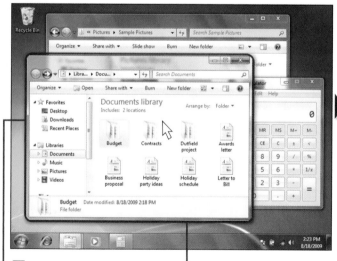

1 If you see the window you want to work with, click anywhere inside the window.

■ The window will appear in front of all other windows. You can now clearly view the contents of the window.

2 To glance through all the windows you have open, move the mouse ▷ over the icons on the taskbar.

■ When you move the mouse ▷ over an icon, a small preview of each open window in the program will appear.

Tip

Does the taskbar offer any visual clues about my programs?

Yes. If a program has an open window, a border will appear around the program's icon on the taskbar. If a program has more than one window open, more than one line will appear to the right of the program's icon on the taskbar.

Tip

Do some preview windows offer special features?

Yes. Some preview windows offer special features. For example, when playing a song in Windows Media Player, the preview window displays playback controls that you can click to play the previous song (▐◀), play the next song (▶▌) or pause the song (▐▐).

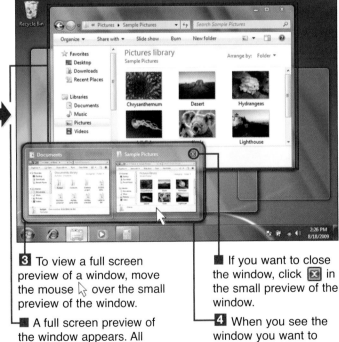

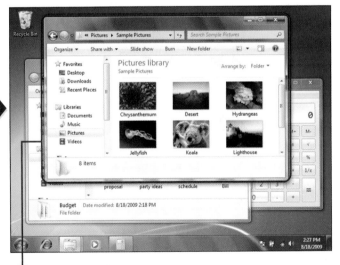

3 To view a full screen preview of a window, move the mouse ▷ over the small preview of the window.

■ A full screen preview of the window appears. All other windows will appear transparent.

■ If you want to close the window, click ⊠ in the small preview of the window.

4 When you see the window you want to work with, click the small preview of the window.

■ The window will appear in front of all other windows.

27

DISPLAY TWO WINDOWS SIDE BY SIDE

You can display two windows side by side on your screen. This allows you to easily review the contents of both windows at the same time.

Displaying two windows side by side also allows you to easily move and copy information between the windows.

DISPLAY TWO WINDOWS SIDE BY SIDE

1 To display two windows side by side on your screen, position the mouse ⟍ over the title bar of one of the windows.

2 Drag the mouse ⟍ to the left or right edge of your screen.

■ The window snaps into place and is resized to fill half of your screen.

3 Position the mouse ⟍ over the title bar of the other window.

4 Drag the mouse ⟍ to the opposite edge of your screen.

Is there a faster way to display two windows side by side?

Yes. If you have only two windows open on your screen, right-click a blank area on your taskbar and then click **Show windows side by side** on the menu that appears. The windows will appear side by side on your screen. If you have more than two windows open, all of your open windows will appear side by side on your screen.

Is there another way I can display windows on my screen?

Yes. You can cascade your open windows so the windows neatly overlap each other. To cascade your open windows, right-click a blank area on your taskbar and then click **Cascade windows** on the menu that appears.

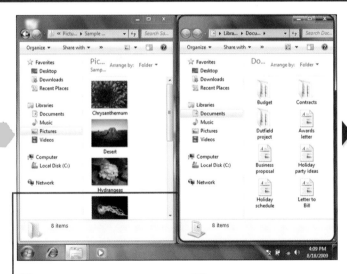

■ The window snaps into place and is resized to fill half of your screen.

■ The windows now appear side by side so you can easily see the contents of both windows at the same time.

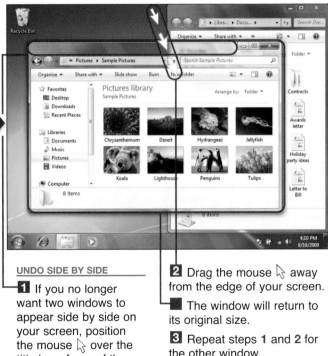

UNDO SIDE BY SIDE

1 If you no longer want two windows to appear side by side on your screen, position the mouse ⃝ over the title bar of one of the windows.

2 Drag the mouse ⃝ away from the edge of your screen.

■ The window will return to its original size.

3 Repeat steps **1** and **2** for the other window.

PUT YOUR COMPUTER TO SLEEP

When you finish using your computer, you can put your computer into a power-saving state known as sleep. When you wake your computer, you will be able to resume working almost immediately.

When sleeping, a computer uses a very small amount of power—about the same amount of power used by a nightlight.

By default, if you do not use your computer for 30 minutes, your computer will automatically go to sleep. A laptop computer will automatically go to sleep after 15 minutes when running on battery power and after 30 minutes when plugged in.

PUT YOUR COMPUTER TO SLEEP

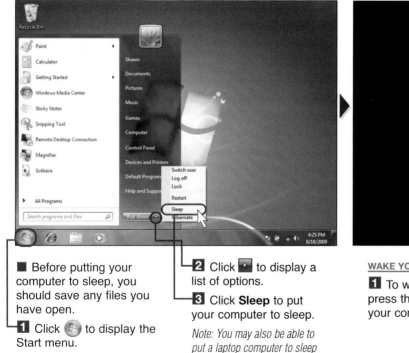

■ Before putting your computer to sleep, you should save any files you have open.

1 Click 🟦 to display the Start menu.

2 Click ▶ to display a list of options.

3 Click **Sleep** to put your computer to sleep.

Note: You may also be able to put a laptop computer to sleep by closing its lid.

WAKE YOUR COMPUTER

1 To wake your computer, press the power button on your computer.

■ You may also be able to click your mouse, press a key on the keyboard or open the lid on a laptop computer to wake your computer. In some cases, pressing the power button may not wake a computer.

If you do not plan to use your laptop computer for an extended period of time, you can put your computer into hibernation. Hibernation is a power-saving state intended mainly for laptop computers.

When you put your computer into hibernation, the computer saves your open documents and programs and then turns off.

When your computer is hibernating, it uses less power than when your computer is asleep.

PUT YOUR COMPUTER INTO HIBERNATION

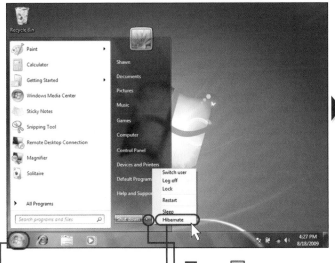

■ Before putting your computer into hibernation, you should save any files you have open as a precaution.

1 Click 🔘 to display the Start menu.

2 Click ▶ to display a list of options.

3 Click **Hibernate** to put your computer into hibernation.

WAKE YOUR COMPUTER

1 To wake your computer, press the power button on your computer.

■ You may also be able to click your mouse, press a key on the keyboard or open the lid on a laptop computer to wake your computer. In some cases, pressing the power button may not wake a computer.

LOCK YOUR COMPUTER

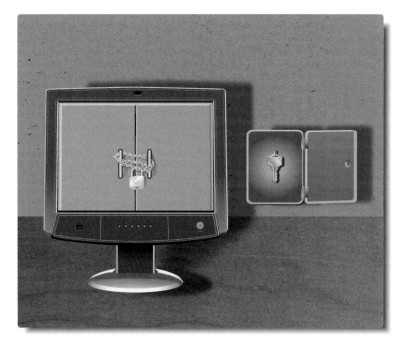

If you will temporarily be away from your computer and want to protect it from unauthorized access, you can instantly lock your computer.

If you want to prevent a colleague or family member from seeing the contents of your computer screen, you can also lock your computer to instantly hide the information on your screen.

To make your computer secure, you should assign a password to your user account. To assign a password to a user account, see page 186.

LOCK YOUR COMPUTER

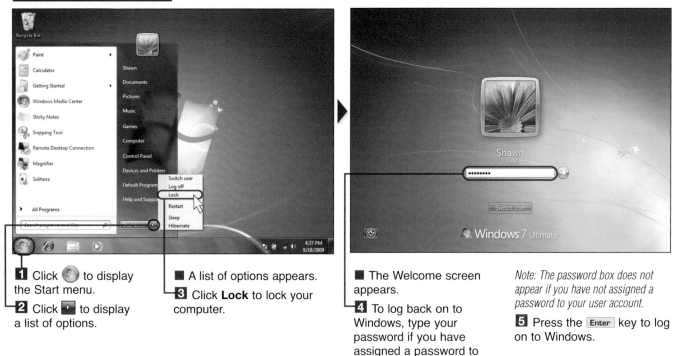

1 Click ⊙ to display the Start menu.

2 Click ▶ to display a list of options.

■ A list of options appears.

3 Click **Lock** to lock your computer.

■ The Welcome screen appears.

4 To log back on to Windows, type your password if you have assigned a password to your user account.

Note: The password box does not appear if you have not assigned a password to your user account.

5 Press the `Enter` key to log on to Windows.

SHUT DOWN WINDOWS

You should shut down Windows when you need to turn off the power to your computer.

For example, shut down Windows before installing new hardware inside your computer or before changing a laptop computer's battery.

SHUT DOWN WINDOWS

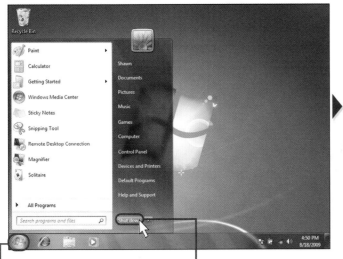

■ Before shutting down Windows, you should save your work and close all the programs you have open.

1 Click 🔵 to display the Start menu.

2 Click **Shut down** to shut down Windows.

■ Windows shuts down and then turns off your computer.

If you do not know how to perform a task in Windows, you can use the Help feature to get help information on the task.

You can also use the Help feature to troubleshoot computer problems.

GET HELP

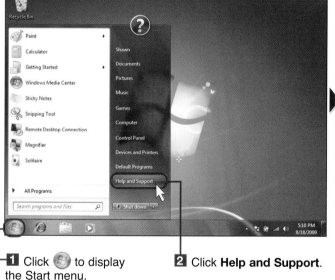

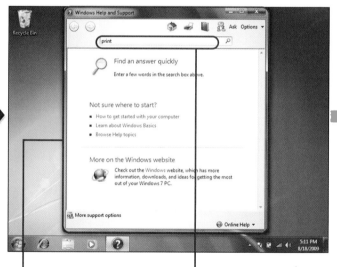

1 Click  to display the Start menu.

2 Click **Help and Support**.

■ The Windows Help and Support window appears, displaying the main help window.

3 To quickly get help information, type a word or phrase that describes the topic of interest. Then press the Enter key.

Tip

Why do many help topics display colored text?

You can click a word or phrase that appears in blue to display information of interest in the current help topic or to display a related help topic. If you click blue text preceded by an arrow (➜), Windows will open the window that allows you to perform the task.

You can click a word or phrase that appears in green to display a definition of the word or phrase. To hide the definition, click outside the definition.

Tip

How can I quickly get help information?

When working in a window or program, you can press the F1 key or click ❓ at the top-right corner of the window or program to get help information. The Windows Help and Support window will appear, displaying help information for the window or program.

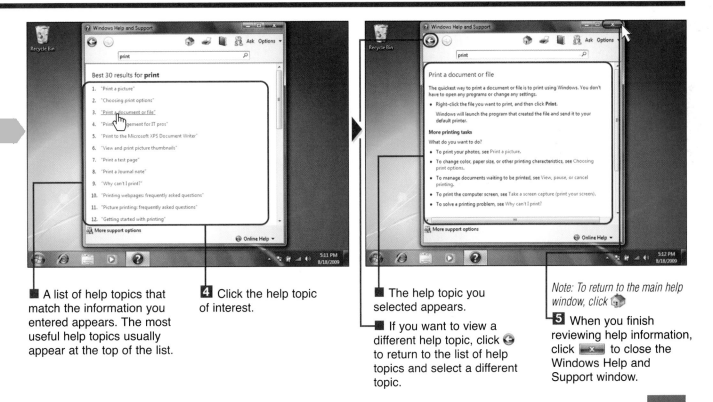

■ A list of help topics that match the information you entered appears. The most useful help topics usually appear at the top of the list.

4 Click the help topic of interest.

■ The help topic you selected appears.

■ If you want to view a different help topic, click ⬅ to return to the list of help topics and select a different topic.

Note: To return to the main help window, click 🔲

5 When you finish reviewing help information, click ✖ to close the Windows Help and Support window.

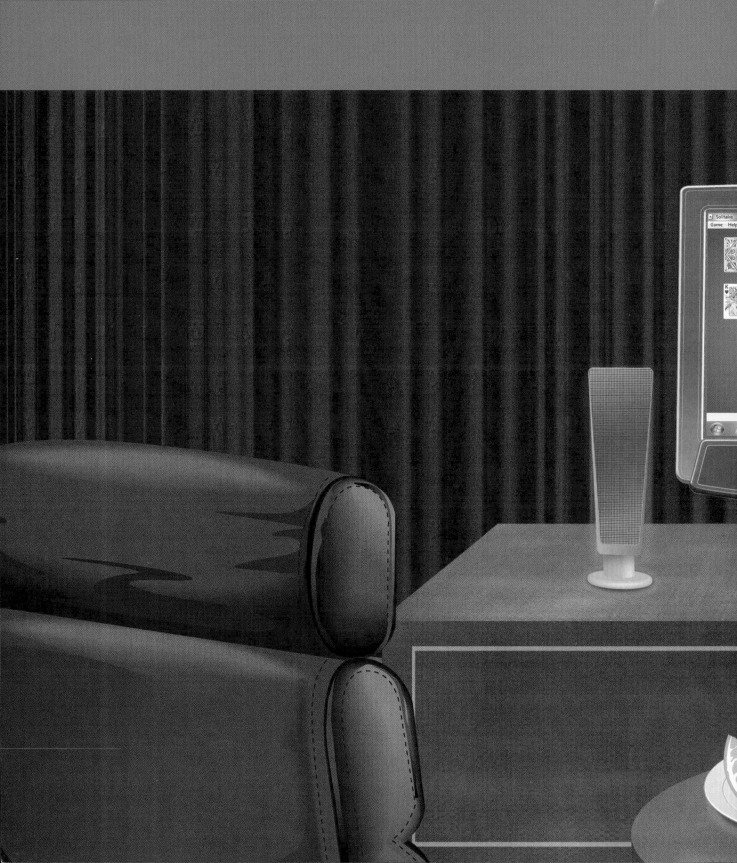

Fun and Useful Programs

CREATE STICKY NOTES

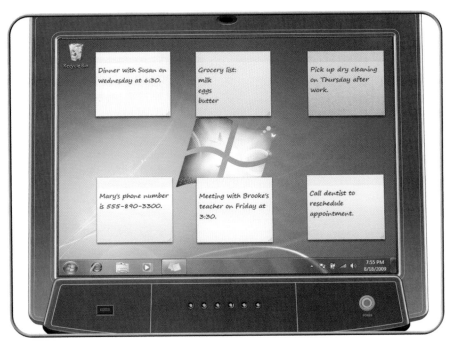

You can create electronic sticky notes that are similar to paper sticky notes.

Sticky notes are useful for storing small pieces of information, such as to-do lists, phone numbers, short notes and reminders. You can create as many sticky notes as you need.

CREATE STICKY NOTES

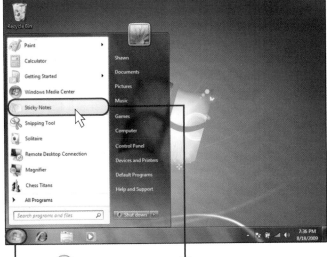

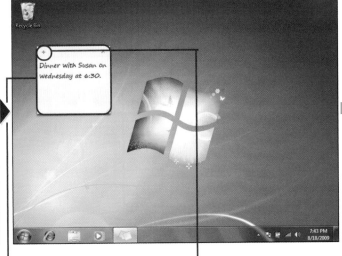

1 Click ⊞ to display the Start menu.

2 Click **Sticky Notes** to create a sticky note.

Note: If Sticky Notes does not appear on the Start menu, click All Programs on the Start menu, then click the Accessories folder and then click Sticky Notes.

■ A sticky note appears.

3 Type the text you want to appear on the sticky note.

■ If you want to create another sticky note, move the mouse ⟋ over the top of the sticky note and then click + .

Tip

Can I change the color of a sticky note?

Yes. To change the color of a sticky note, right-click the note you want to change. On the menu that appears, click the color you want to use for the sticky note, such as Blue, Green, Pink, Purple, White or Yellow. The sticky note will appear in the new color.

Tip

How do I delete a sticky note?

To delete a sticky note you no longer need, position the mouse ⌐ over the top of the sticky note and then click ✕. In the confirmation dialog box that appears, click **Yes** to delete the sticky note.

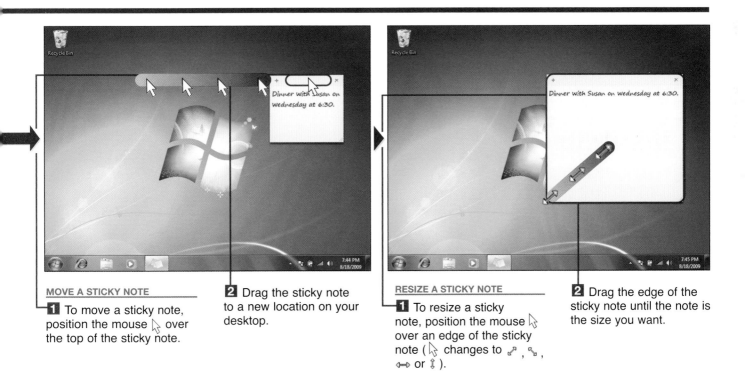

MOVE A STICKY NOTE

1 To move a sticky note, position the mouse ⌐ over the top of the sticky note.

2 Drag the sticky note to a new location on your desktop.

RESIZE A STICKY NOTE

1 To resize a sticky note, position the mouse ⌐ over an edge of the sticky note (⌐ changes to ⤢ , ⤡ , ↔ or ↕).

2 Drag the edge of the sticky note until the note is the size you want.

USING CALCULATOR

Windows provides a calculator that you can use to perform calculations.

You can use Calculator to perform the same calculations you would perform on a handheld calculator.

USING CALCULATOR

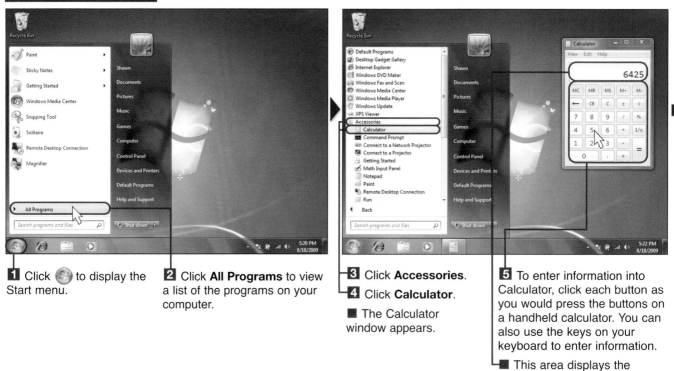

1 Click ⊞ to display the Start menu.

2 Click **All Programs** to view a list of the programs on your computer.

3 Click **Accessories**.

4 Click **Calculator**.

■ The Calculator window appears.

5 To enter information into Calculator, click each button as you would press the buttons on a handheld calculator. You can also use the keys on your keyboard to enter information.

■ This area displays the numbers you enter and the result of each calculation.

Can I enter numbers using the keys on the right side of my keyboard?

Yes. To use the number keys on the right side of your keyboard to enter information into Calculator, the Num Lock light must be on. To turn the light on, press the `Num Lock` key on your keyboard.

What else can Calculator do?

✓ You can use Calculator to convert values from one unit of measurement to another, such as Celsius to Fahrenheit or pounds to ounces. To do so, click **View** in Calculator and then click **Unit conversion** on the menu that appears. An area appears where you can perform unit conversions.

✓ You can also use Calculator to calculate mortgage payments, lease payments and fuel economy. To do so, click **View** in Calculator and then click **Worksheets** on the menu that appears. Click the worksheet you want to use, and an area appears for you to perform the calculation.

*Note: To return to the basic view of Calculator, click **View** and then click **Basic**.*

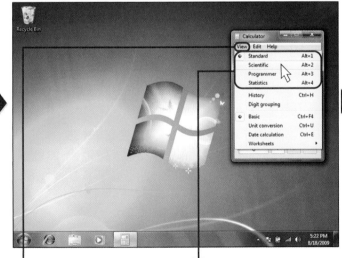

6 To change to a different type of calculator, click **View**.

7 Click the type of calculator you want to use.

■ The calculator you selected appears.

*Note: To return to the Standard calculator, repeat steps **6** and **7**, selecting **Standard** in step **7**.*

8 When you finish using Calculator, click ✕ to close the Calculator window.

CREATE DOCUMENTS WITH WORDPAD

You can use WordPad to create and edit documents, such as letters and memos.

If you need more advanced features than WordPad provides, you can obtain a more sophisticated word processing program, such as Microsoft Word.

CREATE DOCUMENTS WITH WORDPAD

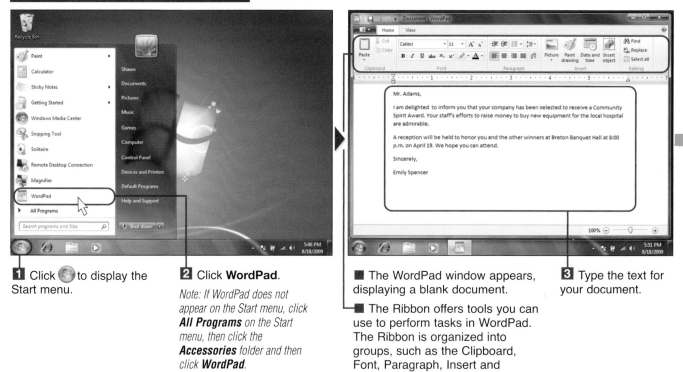

1 Click to display the Start menu.

2 Click **WordPad**.

*Note: If WordPad does not appear on the Start menu, click **All Programs** on the Start menu, then click the **Accessories** folder and then click **WordPad**.*

■ The WordPad window appears, displaying a blank document.

■ The Ribbon offers tools you can use to perform tasks in WordPad. The Ribbon is organized into groups, such as the Clipboard, Font, Paragraph, Insert and Editing groups.

3 Type the text for your document.

Tip

How do I format text in a document?

To format text in a document, drag the mouse I over the text to select the text you want to format. You can then use the following tools to format the text:

Calibri	Change the font of the text.
A˙ A˙	Make the text larger or smaller.
B *I* <u>U</u>	**Bold**, *italicize* or <u>underline</u> the text.
✐ ▾	Highlight the text.
A ▾	Change the color of the text.

Tip

How do I open a document I saved?

To open a document you saved, click ■■▾ at the top-left corner of the WordPad window. In the menu that appears, click the document you want to open in the list of recent documents. If the document you want to open does not appear in the list, click **Open**. In the Open dialog box, click the document you want to open and then click **Open**.

Note: If you are currently working with a document, make sure you save the document before opening another document.

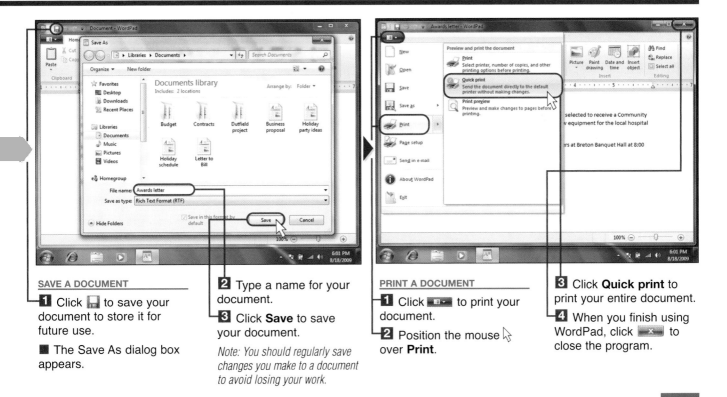

SAVE A DOCUMENT

1 Click 🖫 to save your document to store it for future use.

■ The Save As dialog box appears.

2 Type a name for your document.

3 Click **Save** to save your document.

Note: You should regularly save changes you make to a document to avoid losing your work.

PRINT A DOCUMENT

1 Click ■■▾ to print your document.

2 Position the mouse ☇ over **Print**.

3 Click **Quick print** to print your entire document.

4 When you finish using WordPad, click ✕ to close the program.

DRAW PICTURES WITH PAINT

Paint is a simple program you can use to draw pictures on your computer. You can also use Paint to draw in existing pictures.

If you need more advanced features than Paint provides, you can obtain a more sophisticated graphics program, such as Adobe Photoshop Elements.

DRAW PICTURES WITH PAINT

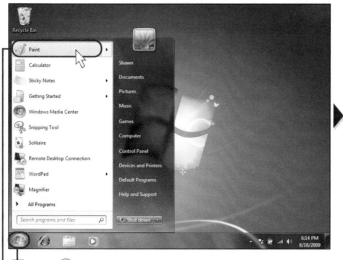

1 Click 🔵 to display the Start menu.

2 Click **Paint**.

*Note: If Paint does not appear on the Start menu, click **All Programs** on the Start menu, then click the **Accessories** folder and then click **Paint**.*

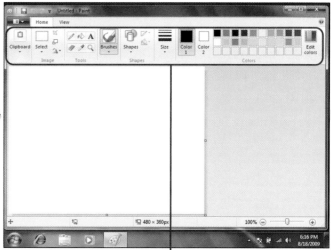

■ The Paint window appears.

■ The Ribbon offers tools you can use to perform tasks in Paint. The Ribbon is organized into groups, such as the Clipboard, Image, Tools, Shapes and Colors groups.

Tip

Can I fill an area with color?

Yes. You can fill a shape with color or
your entire picture. Click the Fill with
color ( ) tool and then click the color
you want to use. Then click inside the
shape you want to fill with color. If you
want to fill your entire picture with
color, click a blank area in your picture.

Tip

Can I cancel a change I made?

Yes. Paint remembers the last
changes you made to a picture. If
you regret a change, you can click the
Undo button ( ) at the top-left
corner of the Paint window to cancel
the last change you made. You can
click the Undo button repeatedly to
cancel previous changes you made.

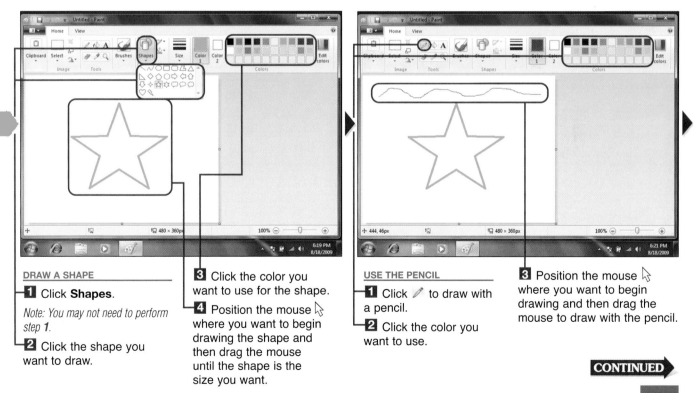

DRAW A SHAPE

1 Click **Shapes**.

*Note: You may not need to perform
step 1.*

2 Click the shape you
want to draw.

3 Click the color you
want to use for the shape.

4 Position the mouse
where you want to begin
drawing the shape and
then drag the mouse
until the shape is the
size you want.

USE THE PENCIL

1 Click to draw with
a pencil.

2 Click the color you
want to use.

3 Position the mouse
where you want to begin
drawing and then drag the
mouse to draw with the pencil.

CONTINUED

47

DRAW PICTURES WITH PAINT

When you finish creating a picture, you can save the picture to store it for future use. Saving a picture allows you to later review and make changes to it.

You should regularly save changes you make to a picture to avoid losing your work.

DRAW PICTURES WITH PAINT (CONTINUED)

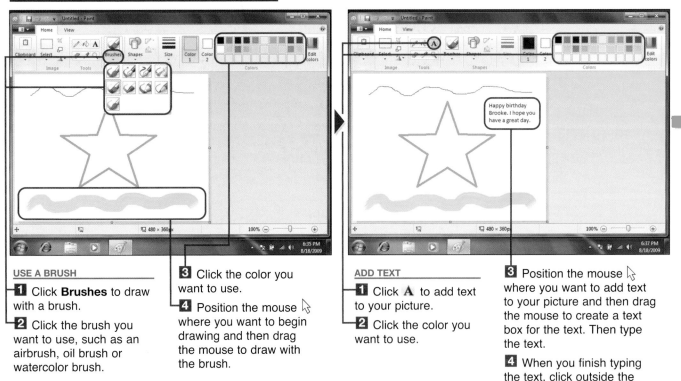

USE A BRUSH

1 Click **Brushes** to draw with a brush.

2 Click the brush you want to use, such as an airbrush, oil brush or watercolor brush.

3 Click the color you want to use.

4 Position the mouse where you want to begin drawing and then drag the mouse to draw with the brush.

ADD TEXT

1 Click **A** to add text to your picture.

2 Click the color you want to use.

3 Position the mouse where you want to add text to your picture and then drag the mouse to create a text box for the text. Then type the text.

4 When you finish typing the text, click outside the text box.

Tip

How do I print a picture?

If you want to print your picture, click ▣▾ at the top-left corner of the Paint window and then click **Print** on the menu that appears. In the Print dialog box, click **Print** to print your picture. Before printing a picture, make sure your printer is turned on and the printer contains paper.

Tip

How do I open a picture I saved?

To open a picture you saved, click ▣▾ at the top-left corner of the Paint window. On the menu that appears, click the picture you want to open in the list of recent pictures. If the picture you want to open does not appear in the list, click **Open**. In the Open dialog box, click the picture you want to open and then click **Open**.

Note: If you are currently working with a picture, make sure you save the picture before opening another picture.

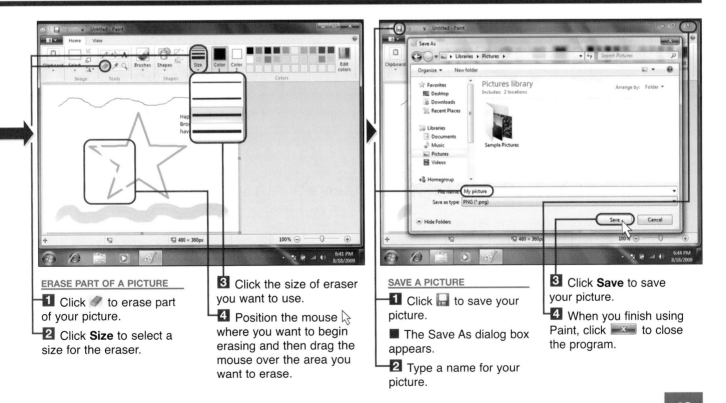

ERASE PART OF A PICTURE

1 Click 🖉 to erase part of your picture.

2 Click **Size** to select a size for the eraser.

3 Click the size of eraser you want to use.

4 Position the mouse ▷ where you want to begin erasing and then drag the mouse over the area you want to erase.

SAVE A PICTURE

1 Click 🖫 to save your picture.

■ The Save As dialog box appears.

2 Type a name for your picture.

3 Click **Save** to save your picture.

4 When you finish using Paint, click ✕ to close the program.

ABOUT WINDOWS LIVE PROGRAMS

You can obtain several free programs at the Windows Live Essentials website (http://download.live.com) to enhance your Windows experience. Some of these programs were previously included in earlier versions of Windows.

Mail

With Mail, you can send and receive e-mail messages. Mail allows you to spell check your messages and saves you time by filtering junk mail you receive. Mail also comes with a calendar that you can use to keep track of your appointments.

Messenger

With Messenger, you can exchange instant messages with friends, family members and co-workers. While chatting, you can share photos and play games. You can even use Messenger to send text messages to a mobile phone.

Writer

With Writer, you can create and update your own personal blog that will serve as your online journal. You can add photos and videos to your blog, format your blog so it looks the way you want and publish your blog to most blog services.

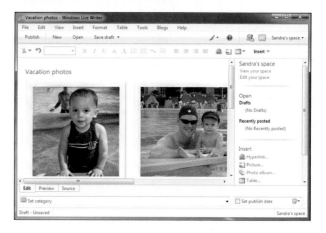

Photo Gallery

With Photo Gallery, you can view and organize your collection of photos and easily share them with family and friends. You can even edit your photos to make them look better.

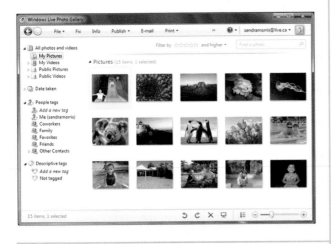

Toolbar

With Toolbar, you can use the new toolbar that will appear at the top of your Internet Explorer window to quickly find what you need. You can preview your Hotmail inbox and photos published by your friends on Windows Live, preview headlines from MSN, quickly perform searches and more.

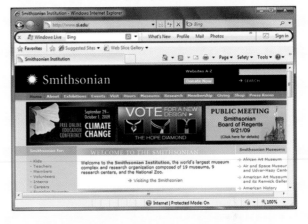

Movie Maker

With Movie Maker, you can create movies using videos and pictures on your computer. You can edit your movies, add music, add visual effects, preview your movies and share your finished movies with family and friends. You can even publish your movies on the web.

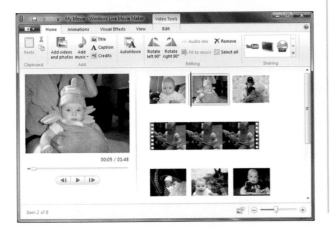

Family Safety

With Family Safety, you can help keep your children safer online. You can block websites, limit searches, monitor the websites your children visit and choose who your children can communicate with.

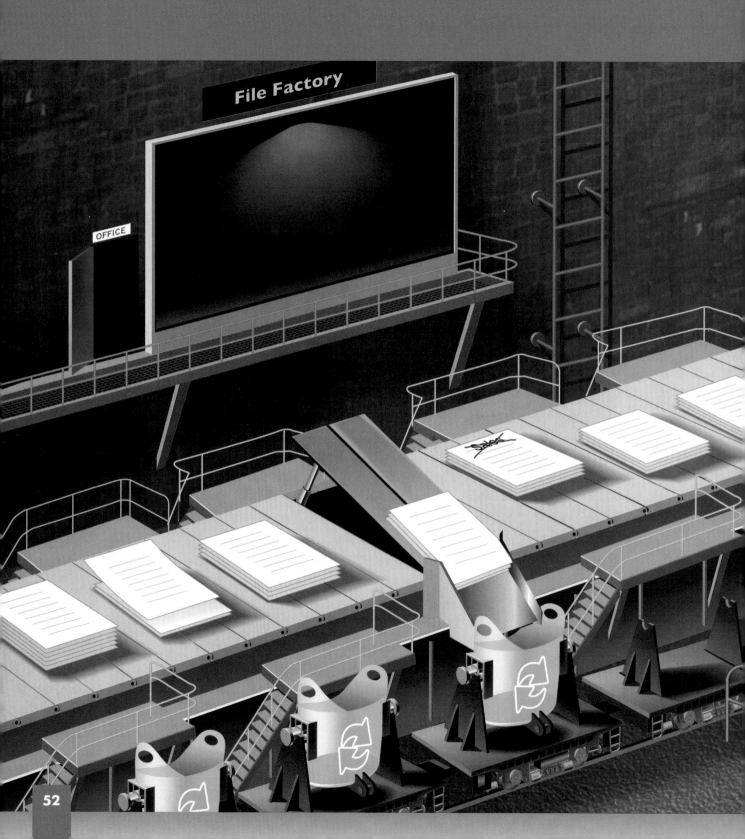

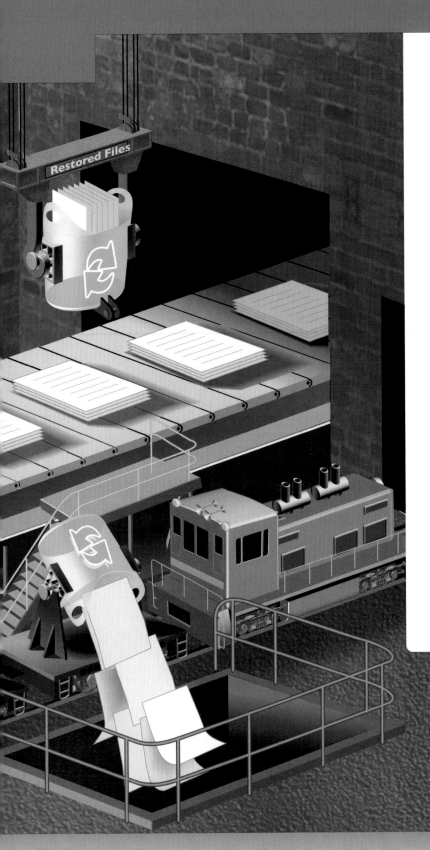

Working With Files

VIEW YOUR FILES

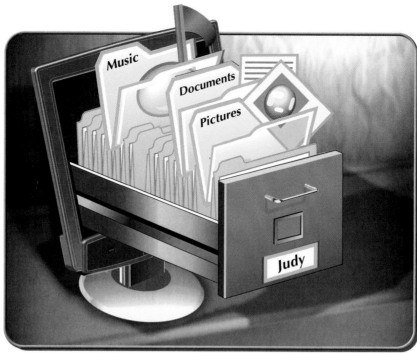

Windows provides several libraries that allow you to easily access and organize your files. You can view the contents of the libraries at any time.

VIEW YOUR FILES

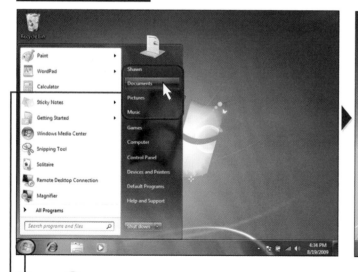

1 Click 🏁 to display the Start menu.

2 Click the library you want to view.

Note: The first item in the list, which displays the name you use to log on to your computer, allows you to view all of your personal folders.

■ In this example, the Documents library appears, displaying your documents.

3 When you finish viewing the contents of the library, click ✕ to close the library.

■ To quickly view all of your libraries, click 📁.

Personal folder

Your personal folder allows you to access all of your personal files and includes the My Documents, My Pictures, My Music and My Videos folders. The name of your personal folder is the same as the name you use to log on to your computer.

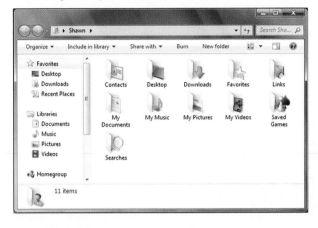

Documents library

The Documents library allows you to access your letters, reports, presentations, spreadsheets and other types of documents. Many programs will automatically save documents you create in the Documents library.

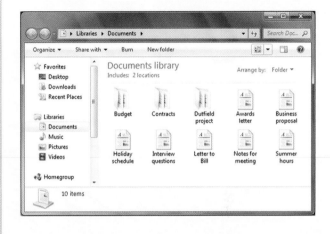

Pictures library

The Pictures library allows you to access your photographs, images and graphics files. Many programs will automatically save pictures you create or edit in this library. When you transfer pictures from a digital camera to your computer, the pictures will appear in the Pictures library.

Music library

The Music library allows you to access music and other sound files. When you copy songs from a music CD to your computer or download music from the Internet, the music often appears in the Music library.

ACCESS DRIVES ON YOUR COMPUTER

You can easily access your hard drive, CDs, DVDs and any other storage devices that are connected to your computer.

ACCESS DRIVES ON YOUR COMPUTER

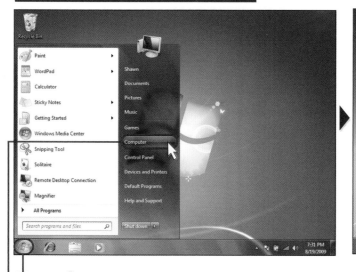

1 Click ![start] to display the Start menu.

2 Click **Computer** to view the drives and other storage devices that are connected to your computer.

■ The Computer window appears.

■ This area displays an icon for your hard drive, which is the primary storage location for programs and files on your computer.

Note: Some computers may display an icon for more than one hard drive.

■ Windows displays the amount of free space and the total amount of space that is available on your hard drive in gigabytes (GB).

Note: Checking the available free space on your hard drive allows you to ensure that your computer is not running out of space.

Tip **What is a USB flash drive?**

A USB flash drive is a small, lightweight storage device that plugs into a USB port on your computer. You can use a USB flash drive to easily transfer information between computers. USB flash drives are also known as memory keys, pen drives, thumb drives and key drives.

Tip **What is a memory card reader?**

Most new computers come with a memory card reader, which is a device that reads and records information on memory cards. Memory cards are most commonly used to transfer information between a computer and an external device, such as a digital camera or video camera.

A memory card reader typically has several slots that allow the reader to accept memory cards from different manufacturers and devices.

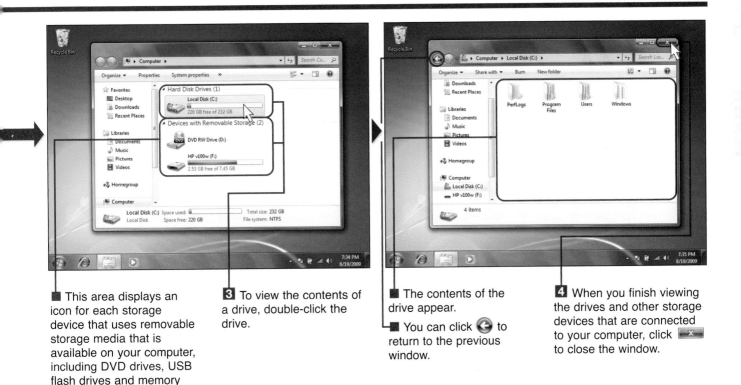

■ This area displays an icon for each storage device that uses removable storage media that is available on your computer, including DVD drives, USB flash drives and memory card readers.

3 To view the contents of a drive, double-click the drive.

■ The contents of the drive appear.

■ You can click ⬅ to return to the previous window.

4 When you finish viewing the drives and other storage devices that are connected to your computer, click ✖ to close the window.

CHANGE VIEW OF FILES

You can change the view of files and folders in a window. The view you select determines the way files and folders will appear in the window.

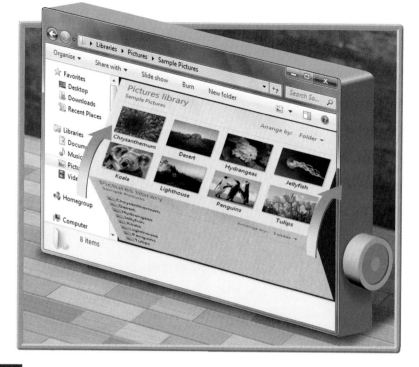

CHANGE VIEW OF FILES

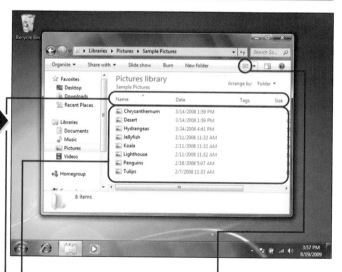

1 Click ▼ on the right side of the Views button to change the view of the files and folders in a window.

■ A list of the available views appears.

2 Click the way you want to view the files and folders in the window.

Note: You can also drag the slider (⬭) to select the way you want to view the files and folders in the window.

■ In this example, the files and folders appear in the Details view.

■ To sort the files and folders in the Details view, click the heading for the column you want to use to sort the files and folders. Click the column heading again to sort the files and folders in the reverse order.

■ To quickly switch between the views, click the left side of the Views button until the files and folders appear the way you want.

THE VIEWS

Extra Large Icons

The Extra Large Icons view displays files and folders as extra large icons.

Large Icons

The Large Icons view displays files and folders as large icons.

Medium Icons

The Medium Icons view displays files and folders as medium-sized icons.

Small Icons

The Small Icons view displays files and folders as small icons.

List

The List view displays files and folders as small icons arranged in a list.

Details

The Details view displays files and folders as small icons and provides information about each file and folder.

Tiles

The Tiles view displays files and folders as medium-sized icons and provides the file type and size of each file and folder.

Content

The Content view displays files and folders as medium-sized icons and shows some of the content of each file for some types of files.

SELECT FILES

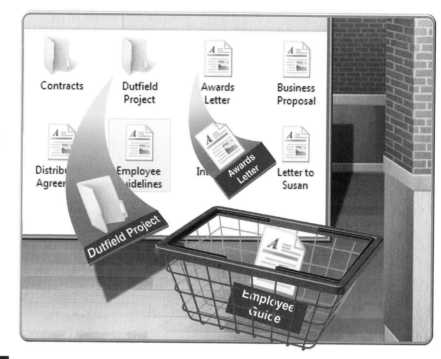

Before working with files, you often need to select the files you want to work with. Selected files appear highlighted on your screen.

You can select folders the same way you select files. Selecting a folder will select all the files in the folder.

SELECT FILES

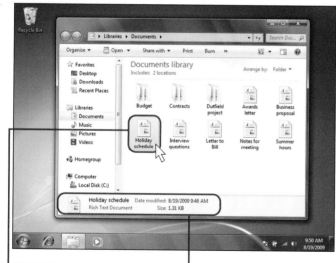

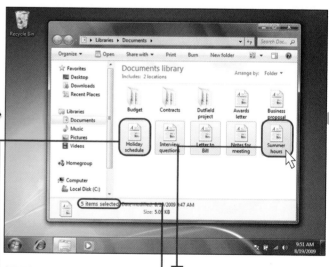

SELECT ONE FILE

1 Click the file you want to select. The file is highlighted.

■ This area displays information about the file, such as the date and time the file was last changed and the size of the file.

Note: The information displayed depends on the type of file you selected.

SELECT A GROUP OF FILES

1 Click the first file you want to select.

2 Press and hold down the Shift key as you click the last file you want to select.

■ This area displays the number of files you selected.

Tip How do I deselect files?

To deselect all the files in a window, click a blank area in the window.

To deselect one file from a group of selected files, press and hold down the `Ctrl` key as you click the file you want to deselect.

Tip Can I select a group of files without using the keyboard?

Yes. To select a group of files without using your keyboard, position the mouse slightly to the left of the first file you want to select. Then drag the mouse diagonally over the files. While you drag the mouse, Windows highlights the files that will be selected. Release the mouse when you finish selecting the files.

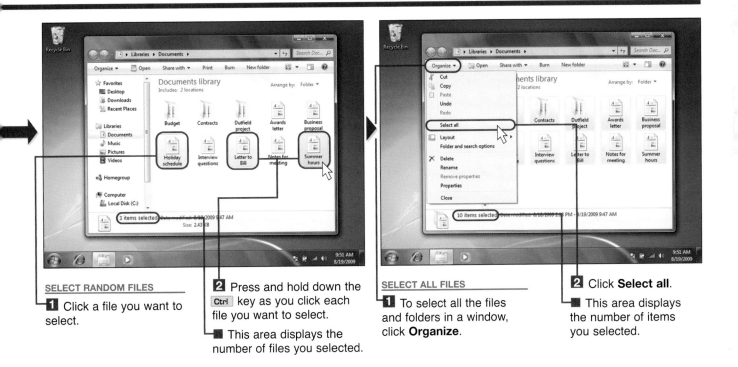

SELECT RANDOM FILES

1 Click a file you want to select.

2 Press and hold down the `Ctrl` key as you click each file you want to select.

■ This area displays the number of files you selected.

SELECT ALL FILES

1 To select all the files and folders in a window, click **Organize**.

2 Click **Select all**.

■ This area displays the number of items you selected.

You can rename a file to better describe the contents of the file. Renaming a file can help you more quickly locate the file in the future.

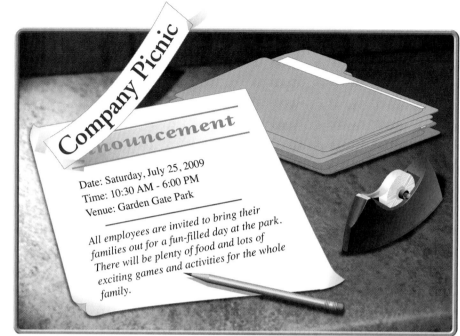

You can rename folders the same way you rename files.

RENAME A FILE

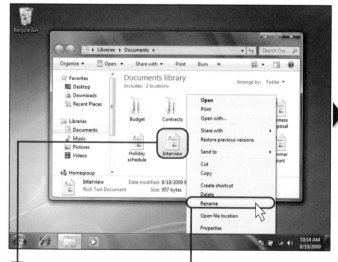

1 Right-click the file you want to rename. A menu appears.

2 Click **Rename**.

Note: You can also rename a file by clicking the file and then pressing the F2 *key.*

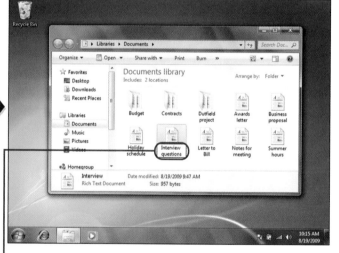

■ A box appears around the file name.

3 Type a new name for the file and then press the Enter key.

*Note: A file name cannot contain the \ / : * ? " < > or I characters.*

■ If you change your mind while typing a new file name, you can press the Esc key to return to the original file name.

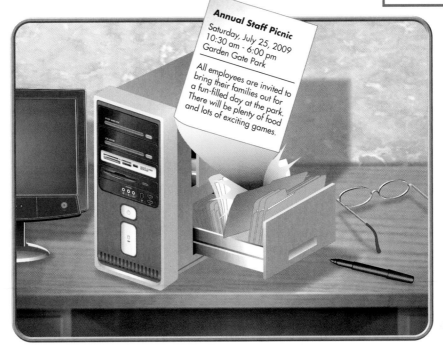

You can open a file to display its contents on your screen. Opening a file allows you to review and make changes to the file.

You can open folders the same way you open files.

OPEN A FILE

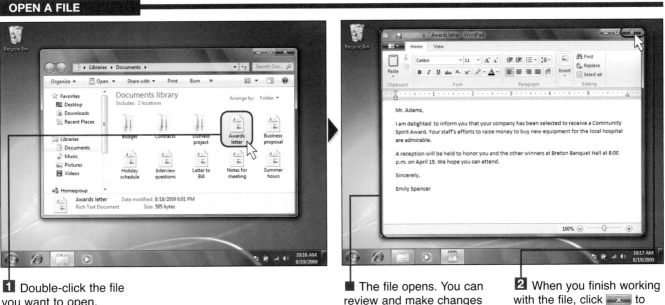

1 Double-click the file you want to open.

■ The file opens. You can review and make changes to the file.

2 When you finish working with the file, click ▅✕▅ to close the file.

OPEN A RECENTLY USED FILE

For each program on your computer, Windows keeps track of the files you have recently used. You can quickly open any of these files.

Windows displays the files you have recently used in lists, known as Jump Lists.

USING THE START MENU

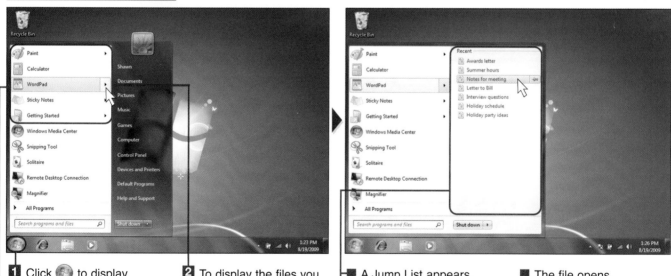

1 Click 🔵 to display the Start menu.

■ An arrow (▶) appears beside the name of each program that offers a Jump List.

2 To display the files you have recently used with a program, click ▶ beside the program name.

■ A Jump List appears, listing the files you have recently used with the program.

3 Click the file you want to open.

■ The file opens.

Tip

Do Jump Lists only show files I have recently used?

Each program offers a unique Jump List. Some Jump Lists also show common tasks. Here are some examples.

Internet Explorer

The Internet Explorer ( ) Jump List shows the webpages you frequently visit.

Windows Explorer

The Windows Explorer ( ) Jump List shows the folders you frequently open.

Windows Media Player

The Windows Media Player ( ) Jump List shows your most frequently played songs, videos and other media. The list also offers options to resume your previous playlist or play all your music.

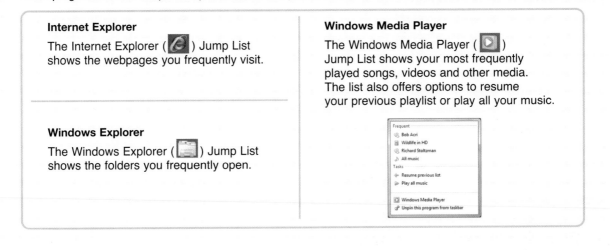

USING THE TASKBAR

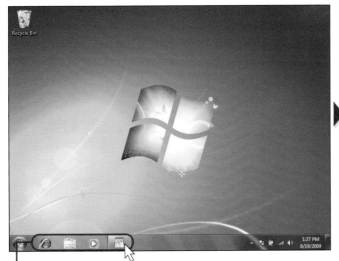

1 To display the files you have recently used with a program, right-click the program's icon on the taskbar.

Note: To add a program's icon to the taskbar to provide a quick way of starting a program you regularly use, see page 162.

■ A Jump List appears, listing the files you have recently used with the program.

2 Click the file you want to open.

■ The file opens.

CREATE A NEW FILE

You can instantly create, name and store a new file in the location you want without starting any programs.

Creating a new file without starting any programs allows you to focus on the organization of your files rather than the programs you need to accomplish your tasks.

CREATE A NEW FILE

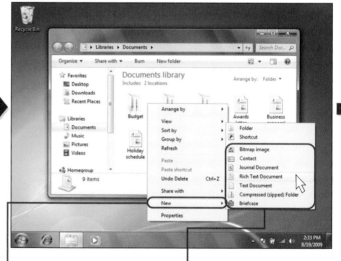

1 Display the contents of the folder or library where you want to create a new file.

■ In this example, we are creating a new file in the Documents library. To view the contents of the Documents library, see page 54.

2 Right-click an empty area in the window. A menu appears.

3 Click **New**.

4 Click the type of file you want to create.

Tip

What types of files can I create?

The types of files you can create depend on the programs installed on your computer.
By default, Windows allows you to create the following types of files.

File Type	Description
Bitmap Image	Creates an image file.
Contact	Creates a contact, which allows you to store a collection of information about a person, such as a person's e-mail address, phone number and street address.
Journal Document	Creates a note you can record in your own handwriting.
Rich Text Document	Creates a document that can contain formatting, such as bold text and colors.
Text Document	Creates a document that cannot contain formatting.
Compressed (zipped) Folder	Creates a folder that reduces the size of the files it contains to save storage space.
Briefcase	Stores files that you want to keep synchronized between two computers, such as a desktop and laptop computer.

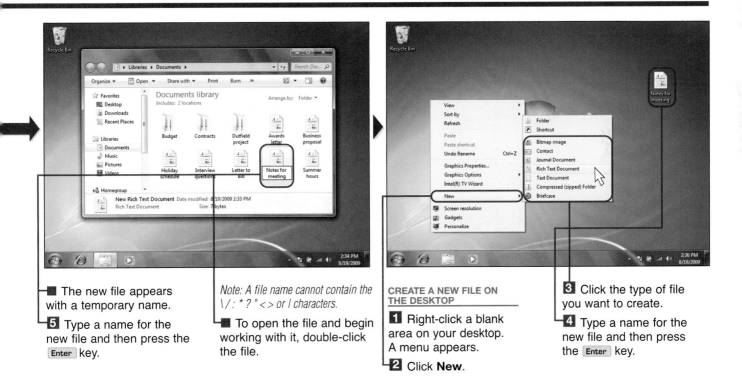

■ The new file appears with a temporary name.

5 Type a name for the new file and then press the `Enter` key.

*Note: A file name cannot contain the \ / : * ? " < > or | characters.*

■ To open the file and begin working with it, double-click the file.

CREATE A NEW FILE ON THE DESKTOP

1 Right-click a blank area on your desktop. A menu appears.

2 Click **New**.

3 Click the type of file you want to create.

4 Type a name for the new file and then press the `Enter` key.

CREATE A NEW FOLDER

You can create a new folder to help you organize the files stored on your computer.

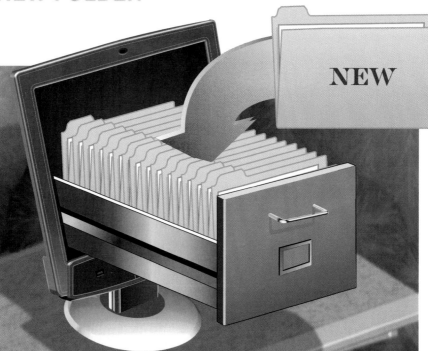

Creating a new folder is useful when you want to keep related files together, such as the files for a particular project.

Creating a new folder is like placing a new folder in a filing cabinet.

CREATE A NEW FOLDER

1 Display the window you want to contain a new folder.

2 Click **New folder**.

*Note: To create a new folder on your desktop, right-click an empty area on the desktop. On the menu that appears, click **New** and then click **Folder**.*

■ The new folder appears, displaying a temporary name.

3 Type a name for the new folder and then press the Enter key.

*Note: A folder name cannot contain the \ / : * ? " < > or | characters.*

You can delete a file you no longer need. The Recycle Bin stores all the files you delete.

Before you delete a file, make sure you will no longer need the file.

You can delete a folder the same way you delete a file. When you delete a folder, all the files in the folder are also deleted.

DELETE A FILE

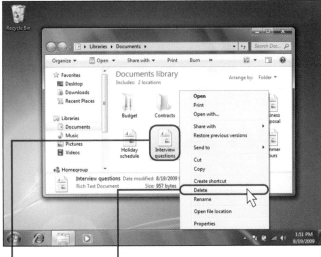

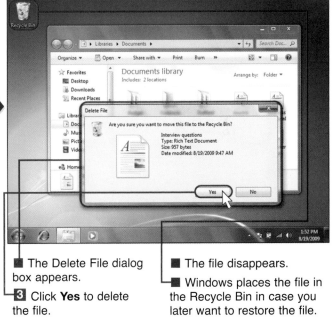

1 Right-click the file you want to delete. A menu appears.

■ To delete more than one file, select all the files you want to delete and then right-click one of the files. To select multiple files, see page 60.

2 Click **Delete**.

Note: You can also delete a file by clicking the file and then pressing the Delete *key.*

■ The Delete File dialog box appears.

3 Click **Yes** to delete the file.

■ The file disappears.

■ Windows places the file in the Recycle Bin in case you later want to restore the file.

Note: To restore a file from the Recycle Bin, see page 70.

RESTORE A DELETED FILE

The Recycle Bin stores all the files you have deleted. You can easily restore any file in the Recycle Bin to its original location on your computer.

You can restore folders the same way you restore files. When you restore a folder, Windows restores all the files in the folder.

You can empty the Recycle Bin to create more free space on your computer. When you empty the Recycle Bin, the files are removed and cannot be restored.

RESTORE A DELETED FILE

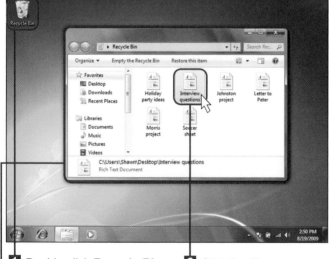

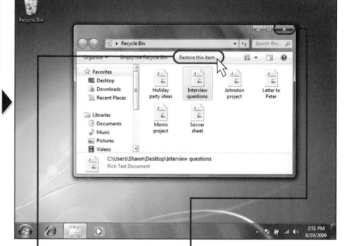

1 Double-click **Recycle Bin**.

■ The Recycle Bin window appears, displaying all the files you have deleted.

2 Click the file you want to restore.

■ To restore more than one file, select all the files you want to restore. To select multiple files, see page 60.

3 Click **Restore this item**.

*Note: If you selected multiple files, click **Restore the selected items** in step 3.*

■ The file will disappear from the Recycle Bin window and return to its original location on your computer.

4 Click ![x] to close the Recycle Bin window.

Tip

Why is the file I want to restore not in the Recycle Bin?

The Recycle Bin may not store files you delete from a location outside your computer, such as a file you delete from a network folder or a USB flash drive. Files deleted from these locations may be permanently deleted rather than placed in the Recycle Bin.

Tip

Can I permanently remove a file from the Recycle Bin?

You may want to permanently remove a file from the Recycle Bin, such as a file that contains confidential information. To permanently remove a file from the Recycle Bin, click the file you want to permanently remove in the Recycle Bin window and then press the Delete key. In the confirmation dialog box that appears, click **Yes** to permanently remove the file.

EMPTY THE RECYCLE BIN

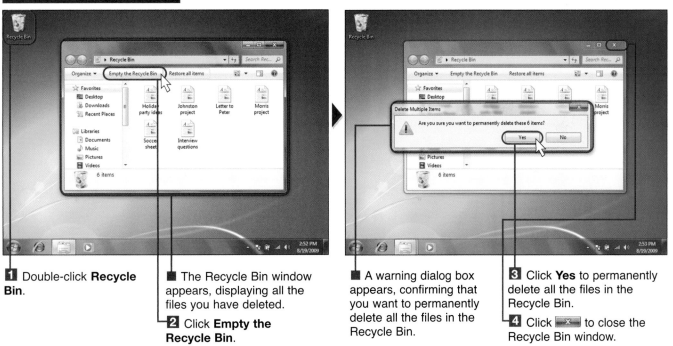

1 Double-click **Recycle Bin**.

■ The Recycle Bin window appears, displaying all the files you have deleted.

2 Click **Empty the Recycle Bin**.

■ A warning dialog box appears, confirming that you want to permanently delete all the files in the Recycle Bin.

3 Click **Yes** to permanently delete all the files in the Recycle Bin.

4 Click ☒ to close the Recycle Bin window.

PRINT A FILE

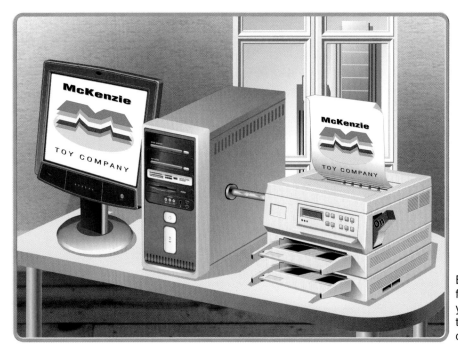

You can produce a paper copy of a file stored on your computer.

Before printing a file, make sure your printer is turned on and contains paper.

PRINT A FILE

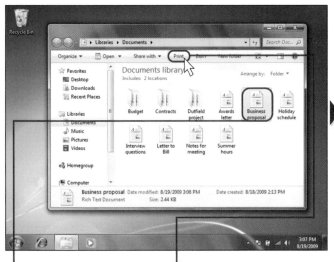

1 Click the file you want to print.

■ To print more than one file, select all the files you want to print. To select multiple files, see page 60.

2 Click **Print**.

Note: If you selected a picture, the Print Pictures dialog box appears. For information on printing pictures, see page 84.

■ Windows quickly opens, prints and then closes the file.

■ When you print a file, a printer icon (🖨) appears in this area. The printer icon disappears when the file has finished printing.

Tip

How can I stop a file from printing?

You may want to stop a file from printing if you accidentally selected the wrong file or if you want to make last-minute changes to the file.

HP Color LaserJet 9500 PCL 6

Printer   Document   View

Document Name	Status	Owner	Pages	Size	S:
Business proposal	Printing	Shawn	3	89.7 KB	3:
Distribution agreeme					3:
Holiday schedule					3:

Printers

⚠ Are you sure you want to cancel the document?

[Yes]   [No]

3 document(s) in queue

1 When viewing the files waiting to print, click the file you no longer want to print and then press the `Delete` key.

2 A confirmation dialog box will appear. You can click **Yes** to stop the file from printing.

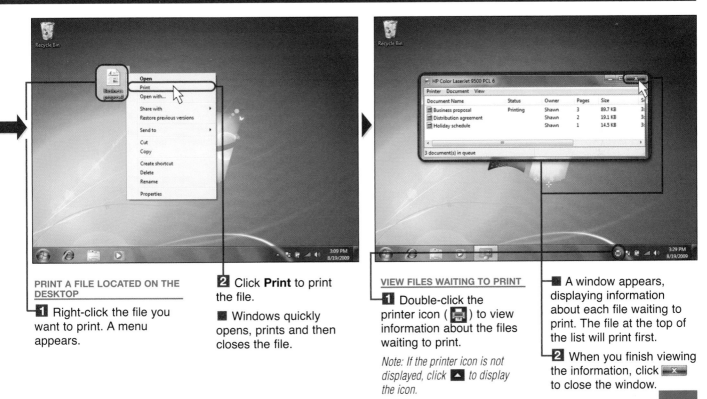

PRINT A FILE LOCATED ON THE DESKTOP

1 Right-click the file you want to print. A menu appears.

2 Click **Print** to print the file.

■ Windows quickly opens, prints and then closes the file.

VIEW FILES WAITING TO PRINT

1 Double-click the printer icon (🖶) to view information about the files waiting to print.

Note: If the printer icon is not displayed, click ▲ to display the icon.

■ A window appears, displaying information about each file waiting to print. The file at the top of the list will print first.

2 When you finish viewing the information, click ✕ to close the window.

MOVE OR COPY A FILE

You can move or copy a file to a new location on your computer.

When you move a file, the file will disappear from its original location and appear in the new location.

When you copy a file, the file appears in both the original and new locations.

You can move or copy a folder the same way you move or copy a file. When you move or copy a folder, all the files in the folder are also moved or copied.

MOVE A FILE

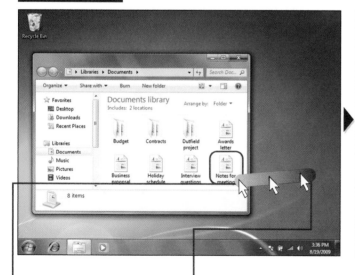

■ Before moving a file, make sure you can clearly see the location where you want to move the file.

1 Position the mouse over the file you want to move.

■ To move more than one file at once, select all the files you want to move. Then position the mouse over one of the files. To select multiple files, see page 60.

2 Drag the file to a new location.

■ The file moves to the new location.

■ The file disappears from its original location.

Tip **Why would I want to move or copy a file?**

You may want to move a file to a different
folder to keep related files in one location.
For example, you can move all the files for
a particular project to the same folder. You
may want to copy a file before you make
major changes to the file. This will give you
two copies of the file—the original file and a
file that you can change.

Tip **How can I make it easier to move or copy
a file?**

Before you move or copy a file from one
window to another window, you may want
to display the two windows side by side on
your screen. This allows you to clearly see
the contents of both windows at the same
time so you can more easily move or copy
a file between the windows. To display two
windows side by side, see page 28.

COPY A FILE

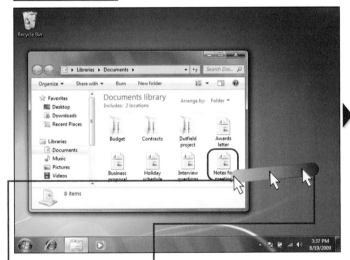

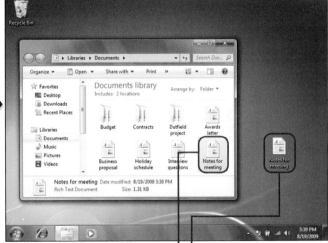

■ Before copying a
file, make sure you can
clearly see the location
where you want to
copy the file.

1 Position the
mouse ⊳ over the file
you want to copy.

■ To copy more than one file
at once, select all the files you
want to copy. Then position the
mouse ⊳ over one of the files. To
select multiple files, see page 60.

2 Press and hold down the
Ctrl key as you drag the file to
a new location.

3 Release the left
mouse button and then
the Ctrl key.

■ A copy of the file
appears in the new
location.

■ The original file remains
in the original location.

If you do not remember where you stored a file on your computer, you can have Windows search for the file.

As you create files on your computer, Windows updates an index to keep track of your files. The index is similar to an index you would find at the back of a book.

When you want to find a file on your computer, Windows scans the index instead of searching your entire computer. This allows Windows to perform very fast searches.

SEARCH FOR FILES

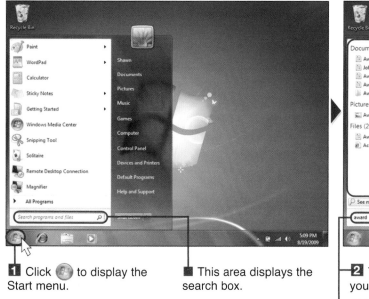

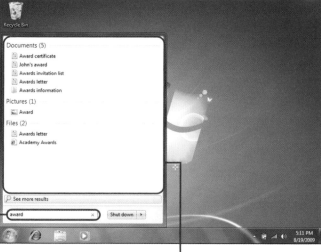

1 Click ● to display the Start menu.

■ This area displays the search box.

2 Type the word or phrase you want to search for.

■ You can type all or part of a file name or a word or phrase that appears within a file.

■ As you type, the names of the matching files that Windows finds immediately appear on the Start menu. Windows organizes the files into categories.

Tip

What types of files can Windows search for?

Windows will search your personal files, including the files in your Documents, Pictures and Music libraries, as well as the files on your desktop. Windows will also search your e-mail messages, your list of favorite webpages and the programs available on your computer. Since Windows searches the programs on your computer, typing a program name into the search box provides a quick way to find a program.

Tip

Can I search for files in a window?

Yes. Searching for files in a window is useful when a window displays many files. In the window you want to search, click in the search box at the top-right corner of the window and then type the word or part of the word you want to search for. As you type, the window immediately displays the matching files that Windows finds.

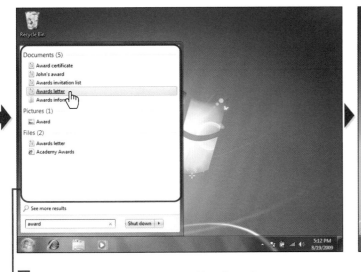

3 If Windows found the file you want to work with, click the file to open it.

Note: If you do not want to open a file, click outside the Start menu to close the menu.

■ The file you selected opens.

ADD A SHORTCUT TO THE DESKTOP

You can add a shortcut to your desktop to provide a quick way of opening a file you regularly use.

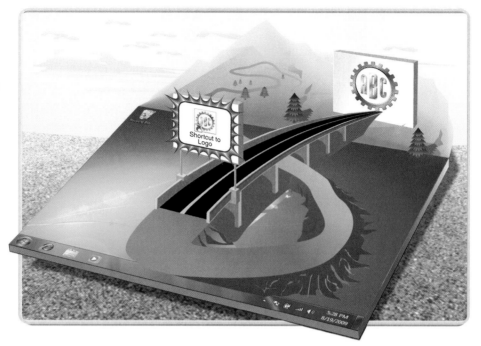

ADD A SHORTCUT TO THE DESKTOP

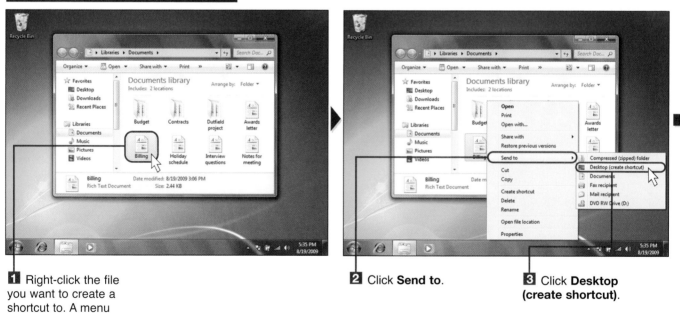

1 Right-click the file you want to create a shortcut to. A menu appears.

2 Click **Send to**.

3 Click **Desktop (create shortcut)**.

Tip

How do I rename or delete a shortcut?

You can rename or delete a shortcut the same way you would rename or delete a file. Renaming or deleting a shortcut will not affect the original file.

✓ To rename a shortcut, click the shortcut and then press the F2 key. Type a new name for the shortcut and then press the Enter key.

✓ To delete a shortcut, click the shortcut and then press the Delete key. In the dialog box that appears, click **Yes** to delete the shortcut.

Tip

Can I move a shortcut?

Yes. If you do not want a shortcut to appear on your desktop, you can move the shortcut to a different location on your computer. You can move a shortcut the same way you would move a file. To move a shortcut, position the mouse over the shortcut and then drag it to a new location.

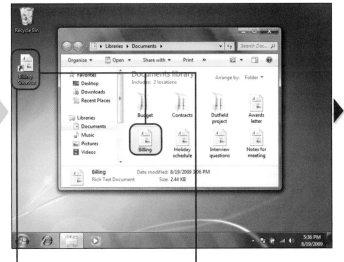

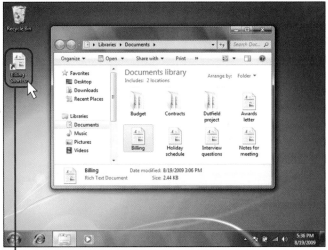

■ The shortcut appears on your desktop.

■ You can tell the difference between the shortcut and the original file because the shortcut icon displays an arrow ( ).

■ You can double-click the shortcut to open the file at any time.

Note: You can create a shortcut to a folder the same way you create a shortcut to a file. Creating a shortcut to a folder will give you quick access to all the files in the folder.

COPY FILES TO A USB FLASH DRIVE

You can copy files stored on your computer to a USB flash drive.

Copying files to a USB flash drive is useful when you want to transfer files between computers. For example, you may want to transfer files between your home and work computers or give a copy of a file to a friend, family member or colleague.

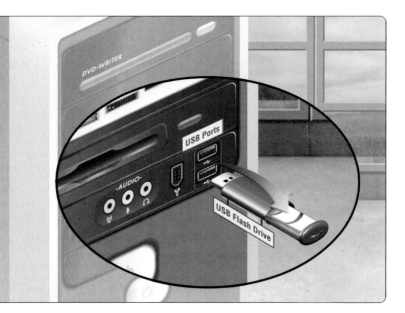

A USB flash drive is a small, lightweight storage device that plugs into a USB port on your computer. A USB flash drive is also known as a memory key, pen drive, thumb drive or key drive.

COPY FILES TO A USB FLASH DRIVE

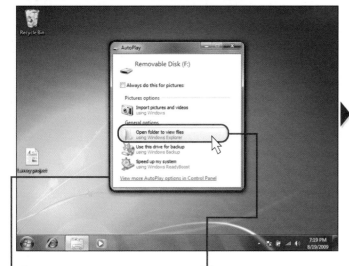

1 Insert a USB flash drive into your computer's USB port.

■ The AutoPlay window appears, listing options that you can select.

2 Click **Open folder to view files** to view the files stored on the USB flash drive.

■ A window appears, displaying the contents of the USB flash drive.

■ This area displays the folders and files stored on the USB flash drive.

Tip

How do I copy files stored on a USB flash drive to my computer?

If you want to copy files stored on a USB flash drive to your computer, perform the steps below, except drag the files from the USB flash drive to your computer. Windows will place copies of the files on your computer.

Tip

How can I safely remove a USB flash drive from my computer?

Before you remove a USB flash drive from your computer, make sure you close any files you have open on the USB flash drive. To safely remove the USB flash drive, click the Safely Remove Hardware and Eject Media icon ( ) at the bottom-right corner of your screen. On the list of devices that appears, click the device you want to remove. A message will appear, indicating that you can safely remove the device.

Note: If you do not see the icon at the bottom-right corner of your screen, click to display the icon.

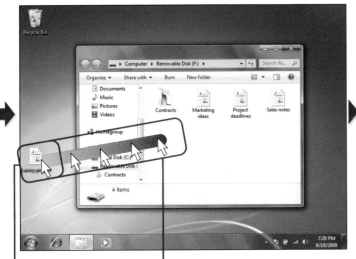

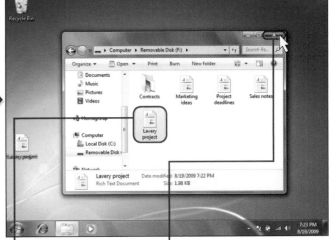

3 Locate the file on your computer that you want to copy to the USB flash drive.

4 Position the mouse over the file.

■ To copy more than one file at once, select all the files you want to copy. Then position the mouse over one of the files. To select multiple files, see page 60.

5 Drag the file to the window displaying the contents of the USB flash drive.

■ Windows places a copy of the file on the USB flash drive.

6 Click to close the window displaying the contents of the USB flash drive.

■ You can now use the USB flash drive to transfer the file to another computer.

PRINT PICTURES

You can print the pictures stored on your computer.

Printing pictures is especially useful when you want to print photos you transferred from a digital camera to your computer.

PRINT PICTURES

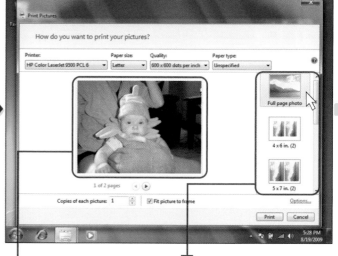

1 Click the picture you want to print.

■ To print more than one picture, select all the pictures you want to print. To select multiple pictures, see page 60.

2 Click **Print** to print the pictures.

■ The Print Pictures dialog box appears.

■ This area displays a preview of the first page that will print.

3 Click the layout you want to use to print your pictures. You can choose to print one or many pictures on each page.

Note: You can use the scroll bar to browse through the available layout options.

Tip

How can I get the best results when printing pictures?

The type of paper you use to print your pictures can significantly affect the quality of the pictures you print. For the best results when printing pictures, use a premium glossy or matte photo paper that is specifically designed for use with your printer. In the Print Pictures dialog box, you can click the area below **Paper type** and select the type of paper you are using.

Tip

Why do my printed pictures look blurry?

If your original pictures are clear but your printed pictures look blurry, you are most likely printing the pictures too large. Try printing your pictures at a smaller size. For the best results when printing pictures, make sure you use the appropriate megapixel setting on your digital camera for the print size you want to use. For example, 8 × 10 prints require at least a 7-megapixel setting, 5 × 7 prints require at least a 3-megapixel setting and 4 × 6 prints require at least a 2-megapixel setting.

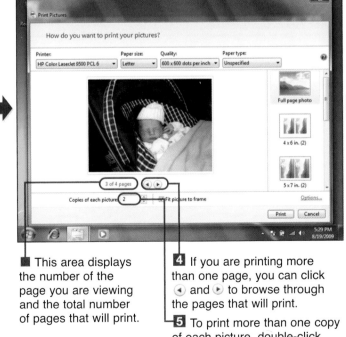

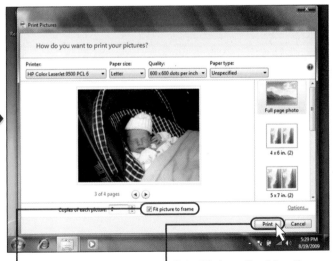

■ This area displays the number of the page you are viewing and the total number of pages that will print.

4 If you are printing more than one page, you can click ◄ and ► to browse through the pages that will print.

5 To print more than one copy of each picture, double-click this area and type the number of copies of each picture that you want to print.

6 This option enlarges the pictures to remove the blank border that may appear around the printed pictures. When this option is on, the edges of the pictures may be cut off. To turn the option on (☑) or off (☐), click the option.

Note: Windows offers this option because digital pictures usually do not match standard print sizes.

7 To print the pictures, click **Print**.

COPY PICTURES FROM A DIGITAL CAMERA

You can copy pictures stored on a digital camera to your computer.

If your camera has a memory card that is compatible with your computer's memory card reader, you can use the memory card to transfer the pictures to your computer.

After copying pictures to your computer, you can work with them as you would any pictures on your computer. For example, you can print, edit or e-mail the pictures.

COPY PICTURES FROM A DIGITAL CAMERA

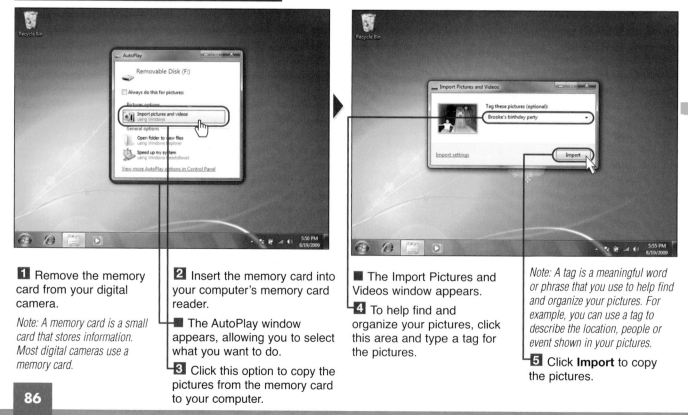

1 Remove the memory card from your digital camera.

Note: A memory card is a small card that stores information. Most digital cameras use a memory card.

2 Insert the memory card into your computer's memory card reader.

■ The AutoPlay window appears, allowing you to select what you want to do.

3 Click this option to copy the pictures from the memory card to your computer.

■ The Import Pictures and Videos window appears.

4 To help find and organize your pictures, click this area and type a tag for the pictures.

Note: A tag is a meaningful word or phrase that you use to help find and organize your pictures. For example, you can use a tag to describe the location, people or event shown in your pictures.

5 Click **Import** to copy the pictures.

Tip

Is there another way to copy pictures from a digital camera?

Yes. You can use a USB cable to connect your digital camera directly to your computer, and then copy pictures from the camera to your computer. After connecting the camera to your computer, turn your camera on and then perform steps **3** to **7** below to copy pictures from the camera to your computer.

Tip

Where does Windows place the pictures I copied from my digital camera?

When you copy pictures from your digital camera to your computer, Windows creates a new folder to store the pictures and places the folder in your Pictures library. Windows names the folder using the date you copied the pictures and the tag you entered. To display the Pictures library, see page 54.

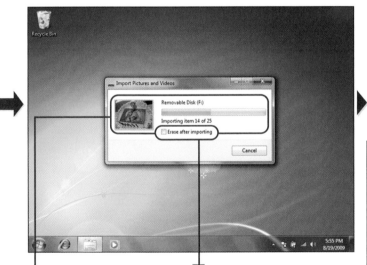

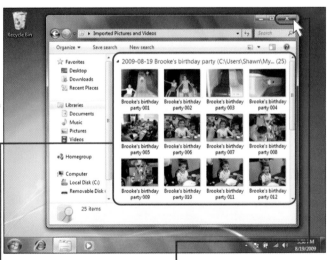

■ This area displays the progress of the copy and a small version of each picture that is being copied to your computer.

6 If you want Windows to erase the pictures from your camera when the copy is complete, click this option (☐ changes to ☑).

■ When the copy is complete, a window appears, displaying the pictures.

■ Windows uses the tag you entered to name each picture.

7 When you finish viewing the pictures, click ✕ to close the window.

Note: To safely remove the memory card from your computer, follow the steps described at the top of page 81.

You can use Windows DVD Maker to quickly and easily create DVDs that can include your favorite videos, pictures and music.

Windows DVD Maker allows you to create DVDs to show your favorite videos as well as create slide shows of your favorite pictures.

After you create a DVD, you can watch the DVD on a television or computer.

COPY PICTURES AND VIDEOS TO A DVD

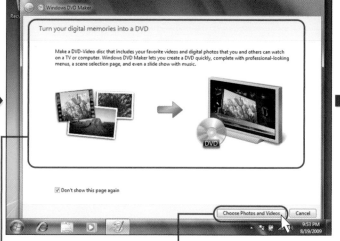

1 Click 🟦 to display the Start menu.

2 Click **Windows DVD Maker**.

*Note: If Windows DVD Maker does not appear on the Start menu, click **All Programs** on the Start menu and then click **Windows DVD Maker**.*

■ The Windows DVD Maker window appears.

■ The first time you start Windows DVD Maker, the window displays information about making DVDs.

3 Click **Choose Photos and Videos** to select the pictures and videos you want to include on the DVD.

Tip

Can I add more than one picture or video at a time?

Yes. In the Add Items to DVD dialog box, press and hold down the `Ctrl` key as you click each picture or video you want to add. Then click **Add** to add all of the pictures or videos you selected.

Tip

How do I remove a video or picture I added?

If you no longer want to include a video on your DVD, click the video in the Windows DVD Maker window and then click **Remove items**. To remove a picture, double-click the Slide show folder to display all the pictures in the folder. Then click the picture you want to remove and click **Remove items**. To once again display the Slide show folder, click .

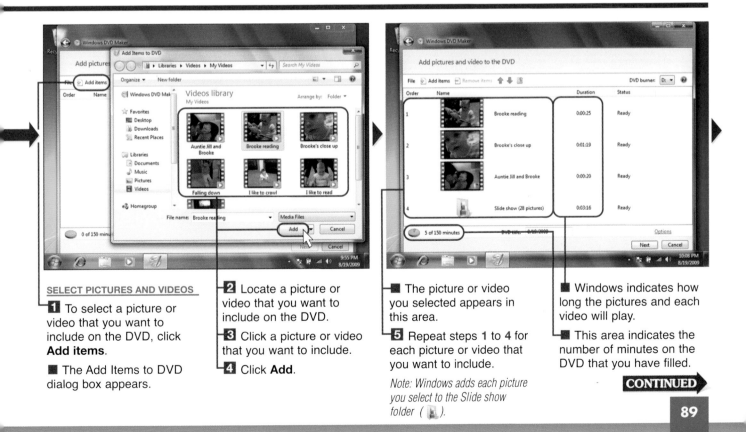

SELECT PICTURES AND VIDEOS

1 To select a picture or video that you want to include on the DVD, click **Add items**.

■ The Add Items to DVD dialog box appears.

2 Locate a picture or video that you want to include on the DVD.

3 Click a picture or video that you want to include.

4 Click **Add**.

■ The picture or video you selected appears in this area.

5 Repeat steps 1 to 4 for each picture or video that you want to include.

Note: Windows adds each picture you select to the Slide show folder (*).*

■ Windows indicates how long the pictures and each video will play.

■ This area indicates the number of minutes on the DVD that you have filled.

CONTINUED

COPY PICTURES AND VIDEOS TO A DVD

When making your DVD, you can change the order of the videos and pictures on the DVD.

You can also specify a title for the DVD that will appear on the DVD's main menu and the style of menu that you want to use.

COPY PICTURES AND VIDEOS TO A DVD (CONTINUED)

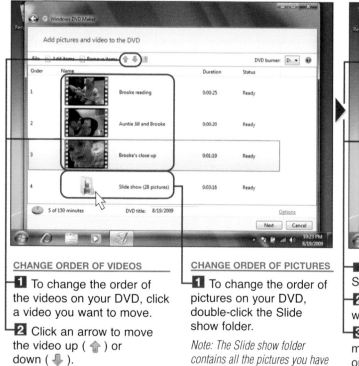

CHANGE ORDER OF VIDEOS

1 To change the order of the videos on your DVD, click a video you want to move.

2 Click an arrow to move the video up (⬆) or down (⬇).

CHANGE ORDER OF PICTURES

1 To change the order of pictures on your DVD, double-click the Slide show folder.

Note: The Slide show folder contains all the pictures you have selected to include on the DVD.

■ The pictures in the Slide show folder appear.

2 Click a picture you want to move.

3 Click an arrow to move the picture up (⬆) or down (⬇).

4 When you finish moving pictures, click 🔼 to once again display the Slide show folder.

Tip

Can I customize the text that appears on the DVD's main menu?

Yes. While creating a DVD, click **Menu text** to customize the DVD's main menu text. You can select a font for the menu text, type a new title for the DVD and type different labels for the Play and Scenes buttons. You can also type notes that viewers can see when they click a Notes button. Changes you make are immediately previewed on the right side of the window. After you finish customizing the text, click **Change Text** to save your changes.

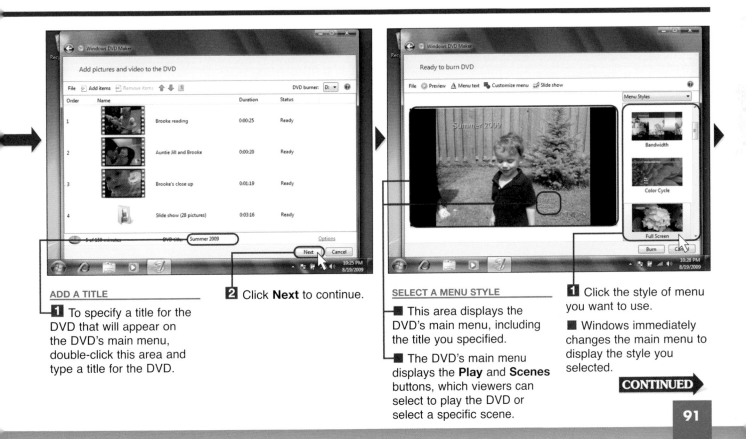

ADD A TITLE

1 To specify a title for the DVD that will appear on the DVD's main menu, double-click this area and type a title for the DVD.

2 Click **Next** to continue.

SELECT A MENU STYLE

■ This area displays the DVD's main menu, including the title you specified.

■ The DVD's main menu displays the **Play** and **Scenes** buttons, which viewers can select to play the DVD or select a specific scene.

1 Click the style of menu you want to use.

■ Windows immediately changes the main menu to display the style you selected.

CONTINUED

COPY PICTURES AND VIDEOS TO A DVD

If you have included pictures on your DVD, you can customize how the pictures will appear in the slide show on the DVD.

You can add music to the slide show and select a transition to specify how you want the slide show to move from one picture to the next.

COPY PICTURES AND VIDEOS TO A DVD (CONTINUED)

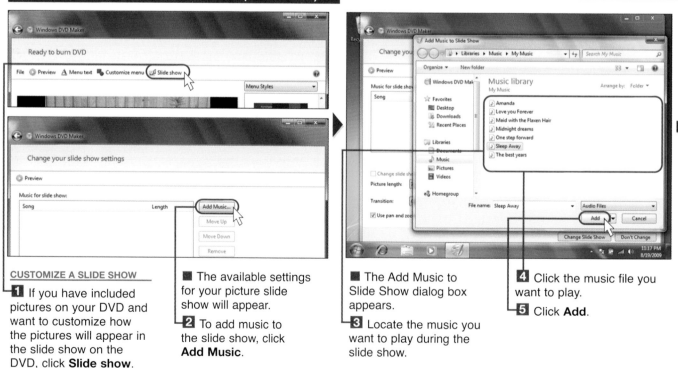

CUSTOMIZE A SLIDE SHOW

1 If you have included pictures on your DVD and want to customize how the pictures will appear in the slide show on the DVD, click **Slide show**.

■ The available settings for your picture slide show will appear.

2 To add music to the slide show, click **Add Music**.

■ The Add Music to Slide Show dialog box appears.

3 Locate the music you want to play during the slide show.

4 Click the music file you want to play.

5 Click **Add**.

Tip

Can I customize the style of the DVD's main menu?

Yes. While creating a DVD, click **Customize menu** to customize the style of the DVD's main menu. You can select a font for the menu text, select a picture or video you want to appear in the foreground and background of the menu, select music to play while the menu is displayed and select a shape for the Scenes button. Changes you make are immediately previewed on the right side of the window. After you finish customizing the main menu, click **Change Style** to save your changes.

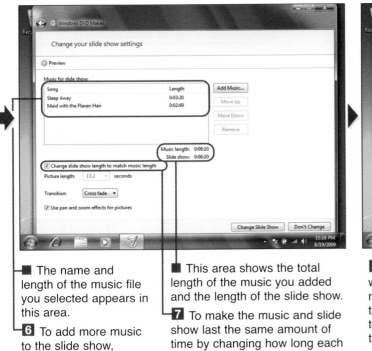

■ The name and length of the music file you selected appears in this area.

■6 To add more music to the slide show, repeat steps **2** to **5** for each music file.

■ This area shows the total length of the music you added and the length of the slide show.

■7 To make the music and slide show last the same amount of time by changing how long each picture appears, click this option (□ changes to ☑).

■8 To select the way you want the slide show to move from one picture to the next, click this area to display the available transitions.

■9 Click the transition you want to use.

■10 Click **Change Slide Show** to save your changes.

COPY PICTURES AND VIDEOS TO A DVD

Before burning a DVD, you can preview how the DVD will play. Previewing a DVD allows you to determine if you need to make any changes to the DVD before burning the DVD.

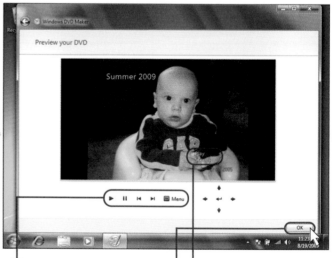

PREVIEW A DVD

1 To preview how the DVD will play, click **Preview**.

■ The preview of the DVD appears.

2 While previewing the DVD, you can click one of the following options:

Play (►) or Pause (❚❚)

Skip to previous (❙◀) or next (▶❙) chapter

Display the main menu (▣)

3 To select a menu option on the DVD, click the option you want.

4 When you finish previewing the DVD, click **OK**.

Tip

Can I save a project I created in Windows DVD Maker?

Yes. At any time while making a DVD, you can save your project so you can later review and make changes to the project. To save a project, click **File** in the Windows DVD Maker window and then click **Save**. Type a name for your project in the dialog box that appears and then click **Save**.

Tip

How do I later open a project I created in Windows DVD Maker?

To later open and work with a saved project you made in Windows DVD Maker, click **File** in the Windows DVD Maker window and then click **Open project file**. In the dialog box that appears, click the project and then click **Open**. You can also open a project you recently saved by clicking **File** in the Windows DVD Maker window and then clicking the name of the project at the bottom of the File menu.

BURN A DVD

■ When you finish creating your DVD, you can burn the videos, pictures and music you selected onto a DVD.

1 Insert a recordable DVD into your recordable DVD drive.

2 Click **Burn** to burn the DVD.

■ A dialog box will appear, showing the progress of the copy.

■ When Windows has finished burning the DVD, a dialog box appears, indicating that the DVD is ready.

■ If you want to make another copy of the DVD, remove the completed DVD, insert a new recordable DVD and then click **Make another copy of this DVD**.

3 To close the dialog box, click **Close**.

Note: To close the Windows DVD Maker window, click ❌ *in the window.*

START WINDOWS LIVE PHOTO GALLERY

You can use Windows Live Photo Gallery to view, organize and edit your photos and videos.

Windows Live Photo Gallery is not included in Windows 7, but the program is available for free at the Windows Live Essentials website (http://download.live.com). For more information on this website, see page 50.

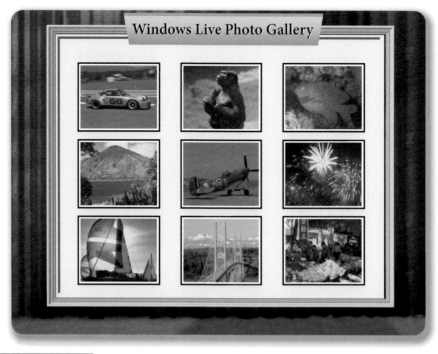

START WINDOWS LIVE PHOTO GALLERY

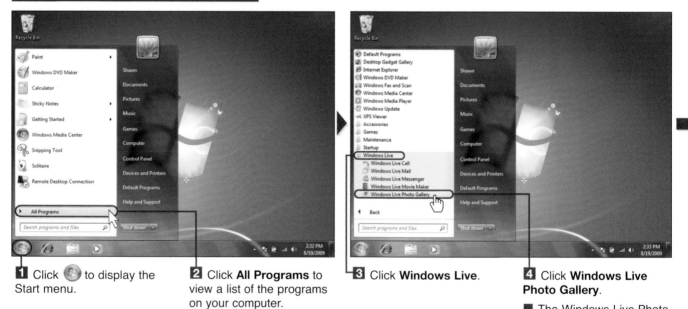

1 Click 🟢 to display the Start menu.

2 Click **All Programs** to view a list of the programs on your computer.

3 Click **Windows Live**.

4 Click **Windows Live Photo Gallery**.

■ The Windows Live Photo Gallery window appears.

Tip

**Do I have to sign in to use Windows
Live Photo Gallery?**

No. You do not need to sign in to use
Windows Live Photo Gallery. However,
signing in gives you access to more
features, such as the ability to share
photos and videos with friends and
family on the web. If you do not want
to sign in, click **Cancel** in the Sign in
dialog box. You can always sign in
later by clicking **Sign in** at the top-right
corner of the Windows Live Photo
Gallery window.

Tip

**How can I see all of my photos or
videos in Windows Live Photo Gallery?**

If you want to see all of your photos or
videos in Windows Live Photo Gallery,
click **My Pictures** or **My Videos** on the
left side of the window. If you want to
see all of the photos or videos shared by
every user on your computer, click
Public Pictures or **Public Videos**. For
information on sharing photos and
videos with other users, see page 188.

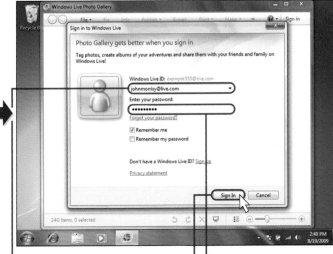

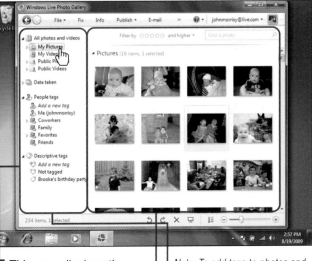

■ When you first start
Windows Live Photo Gallery,
a dialog box appears, stating
that Photo Gallery gets better
when you sign in.

5 To sign in, type your
Windows Live e-mail address.

6 Click this area and
type your Windows Live
password.

*Note: If you do not have a
Windows Live ID, you can
click **Sign up** to get one.*

7 Click **Sign In**.

■ This area displays the
categories used to organize
your photos and videos.
You can view your photos
and videos by location, the
date taken, people tag or
descriptive tag.

*Note: To add tags to photos and
videos, see page 98.*

8 Click the category you
want to view.

■ This area displays the
photos and videos in the
category you selected.

MANAGE YOUR PHOTOS

In Windows Live Photo Gallery, you can add tags to your photos to make your photos easier to find and organize.

A tag is a meaningful word or phrase that you can add to your photos. You can also add tags to your videos.

When you copy photos from a digital camera to your computer, Windows allows you to enter a tag that it will add to every photo. For more information, see page 86. You can add more tags to the photos at any time.

CREATE A TAG

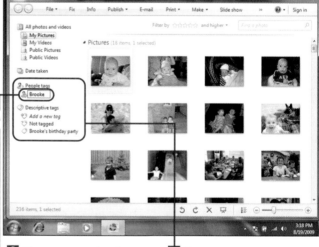

■ In Windows Live Photo Gallery, you can create people tags to identify the people in your photos. You can also create descriptive tags to describe the locations and events in your photos.

Note: To start Windows Live Photo Gallery, see page 96.

1 To create a tag, click **Add a new tag** below the People tags or Descriptive tags category.

2 Type a name for the new tag and then press the Enter key.

■ The tag will appear in your list of tags.

3 Repeat steps **1** and **2** for each tag you want to create.

Tip

Is there a faster way to add tags to photos?

Yes. You can instantly add the same tag to many photos at once. For example, you could add a "graduation" tag to 20 photos of a graduation ceremony. In Windows Live Photo Gallery, press and hold down the `Ctrl` key as you click each photo you want to add a tag to. Then drag the photos to the tag.

Tip

Can I remove a tag I added to a photo?

Yes. If you want to remove a tag from a photo, click the photo in Windows Live Photo Gallery and then click **Info** to display the Info pane. In the Info pane, position the mouse ⌖ over the tag you want to remove from the photo and then click ✕ that appears beside the tag. In the confirmation dialog box that appears, click **Yes** to remove the tag.

*Note: To close the Info pane, click **Info** again.*

ADD TAGS TO PHOTOS

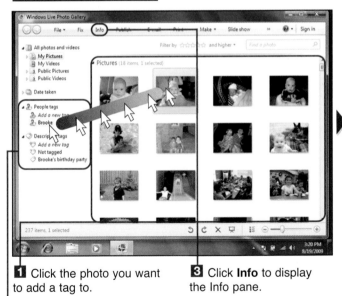

1 Click the photo you want to add a tag to.

2 Drag the photo to the tag you want to add to the photo.

3 Click **Info** to display the Info pane.

■ The Info pane appears, displaying information about the photo, including the tag you added to the photo.

*Note: To close the Info pane, click **Info** again.*

4 If you want to add additional tags to the photo, repeat steps **1** and **2** for each tag you want to add to the photo. You can add as many tags as you want to a photo.

MANAGE YOUR PHOTOS

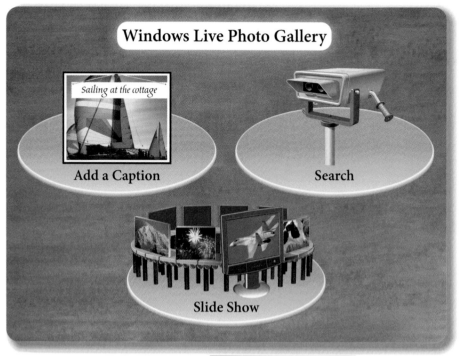

Windows Live Photo Gallery

Add a Caption

Search

Slide Show

With Windows Live Photo Gallery, you can add captions to your photos, search for photos and display your photos as a full-screen slide show.

Adding captions to your photos allows you to describe your photos and can help you later find them. You can also add captions to videos as well as search for videos.

ADD A CAPTION

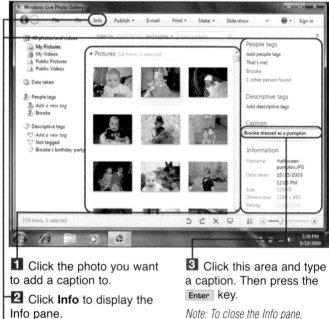

1 Click the photo you want to add a caption to.

2 Click **Info** to display the Info pane.

■ The Info pane appears, displaying information about the photo.

3 Click this area and type a caption. Then press the `Enter` key.

*Note: To close the Info pane, click **Info** again.*

SEARCH FOR PHOTOS

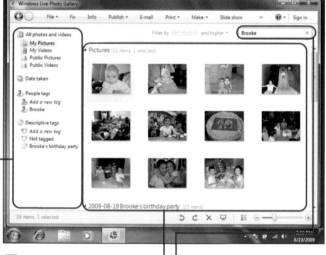

1 Click the category that contains the photos you want to search.

*Note: To search all your photos, click **My Pictures**.*

2 Click this area and type the tag or caption you added to the photo that you want to find.

■ As you type, the matching photos will appear.

Note: To clear a search, click ✕ in the search box.

How can I control my slide show?

When viewing a slide show, there are several controls you can use to control the slide show.

Themes Select a different theme, such as Album, Collage or Travel, to present your photos in a different way.

Pause the slide show

 Display the previous or next photo

Can I share my photos on the web?

Yes. You can place your photos on the web to share them with friends and family. To select the photos you want to share in Windows Live Photo Gallery, press and hold down the Ctrl key as you click each photo. At the top of the window, click **Publish** and then click **Online album** on the menu that appears. Follow the instructions on your screen to publish your photos.

Note: You will need to sign in with your Windows Live ID or obtain a Windows Live ID to share photos on the web.

VIEW A SLIDE SHOW

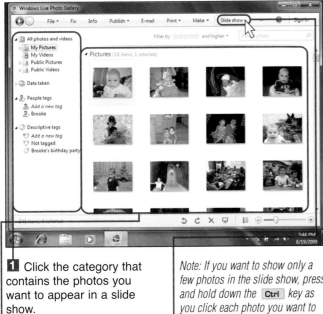

1 Click the category that contains the photos you want to appear in a slide show.

■ This area displays the photos in the category you selected.

Note: If you want to show only a few photos in the slide show, press and hold down the Ctrl key as you click each photo you want to include.

2 Click **Slide show** to start the slide show.

■ The slide show begins. Windows automatically moves from one photo to the next.

3 To display the slide show controls, move your mouse.

Note: When you stop moving your mouse, the slide show controls will automatically disappear.

4 When you finish viewing the slide show, click **Exit**.

EDIT YOUR PHOTOS

You can use Windows Live Photo Gallery to make changes to your photos. For example, you can adjust the exposure and colors in a photo.

EDIT YOUR PHOTOS

1 In Windows Live Photo Gallery, click the photo you want to edit.

Note: To start Windows Live Photo Gallery, see page 96.

2 Click **Fix** to make changes to the photo.

■ A large version of the photo appears.

■ This area displays options you can select to make changes to the photo.

■ As you make changes to the photo, Windows will display a check mark (✓) beside each option that you adjust.

Tip

Can I adjust a photo's exposure and colors myself?

Yes. While editing a photo in the Windows Live Photo Gallery, you can adjust a photo's exposure, adjust a photo's colors or straighten a photo yourself. To do so, click the **Adjust exposure**, **Adjust color** or **Straighten photo** option and then drag the slider ( ) for the setting you want to change. The photo will immediately display the changes you make.

Tip

Can I create panoramic photos?

Yes. You can "stitch" together a series of photos from the same scene to create a panoramic photo. In Windows Live Photo Gallery, press and hold down the Ctrl key as you click each photo you want to include. Click **Make** at the top of the window and then click **Create panoramic photo** on the menu that appears. In the dialog box that appears, type a name for the new photo and then click **Save**. The new panoramic photo will appear.

Note: If you do not see **Make** at the top of the window, click » to display the option.

AUTO ADJUST A PHOTO

1 To have Windows automatically adjust the photo's exposure and colors as well as automatically straighten the photo, click **Auto adjust**.

■ Windows automatically adjusts the photo and displays the exposure, color and straighten photo settings.

2 To browse through the settings, click ∧ or ∨.

3 To hide the exposure, color or straighten photo settings, click the option.

CONTINUED

When editing a photo in the Windows Live Photo Gallery, you can crop the photo to remove parts of the photo you do not want to show or to zoom in on certain parts of the photo. You can also fix red eye.

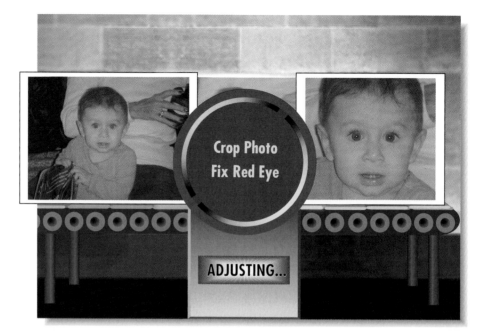

EDIT YOUR PHOTOS (CONTINUED)

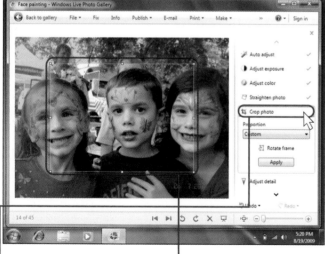

CROP A PHOTO

1 To remove parts of a photo you do not want to show or to zoom in on certain parts of a photo, click **Crop photo**.

■ A frame appears around the photo. Windows will remove the part of the photo that appears outside of the frame.

2 To change the size of the frame, position the mouse ▷ over a box (■) on the frame (▷ changes to ⟺).

3 Drag the mouse ⟺ until the frame includes the part of the photo you want to keep.

4 Repeat steps **2** and **3** until the frame includes the part of the photo you want to keep.

5 Click **Apply** to remove the part of the photo that appears outside of the frame.

Tip

Can I crop a photo to fit in a standard print size?

Yes. While editing a photo in the Windows Live Photo Gallery, you can crop the photo to fit in a standard print size, such as 5 × 7. Click **Crop photo** and then click the area below **Proportion** to select the print size you plan to use. As you change the size of the frame in steps **2** to **4** on page 104, the frame will maintain the correct proportions for the print size you selected.

*Note: If you want to rotate the frame so the frame is tall rather than wide, click **Rotate frame**.*

Tip

Can I undo changes I made to a photo?

Yes. When editing a photo, you can click **Undo** at the bottom of the Windows Live Photo Gallery window to undo your last change. To undo each change you have made, one at a time, click **Undo** more than once. If you later want to undo all of the changes you have made to a photo, click the photo in Windows Live Photo Gallery, click **Fix** and then click **Revert** to return to the original photo. In the confirmation dialog box that appears, click **Revert**.

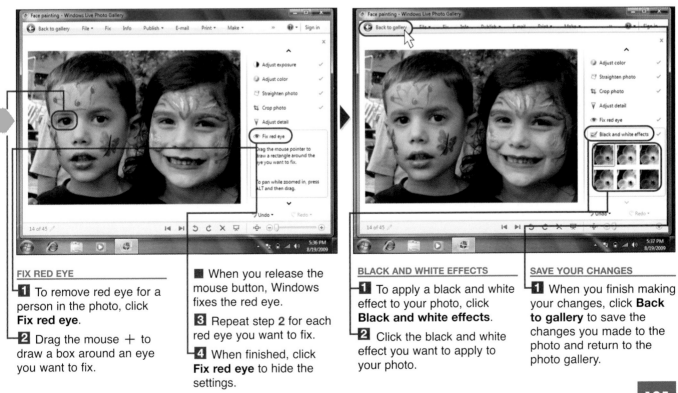

FIX RED EYE

1 To remove red eye for a person in the photo, click **Fix red eye**.

2 Drag the mouse + to draw a box around an eye you want to fix.

■ When you release the mouse button, Windows fixes the red eye.

3 Repeat step **2** for each red eye you want to fix.

4 When finished, click **Fix red eye** to hide the settings.

BLACK AND WHITE EFFECTS

1 To apply a black and white effect to your photo, click **Black and white effects**.

2 Click the black and white effect you want to apply to your photo.

SAVE YOUR CHANGES

1 When you finish making your changes, click **Back to gallery** to save the changes you made to the photo and return to the photo gallery.

Working with Songs and Videos

You can use Windows Media Player to play videos and sounds on your computer.

You can obtain videos and sounds on the Internet or in e-mail messages you receive from friends, family members or colleagues.

You can also obtain videos by transferring video from a video camera to your computer or obtain sounds by copying songs from music CDs to your computer.

PLAY A VIDEO OR SOUND

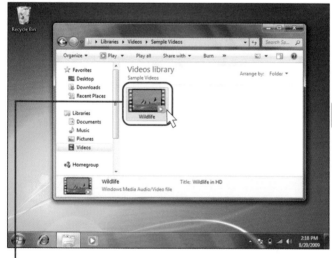

1 Double-click the video or sound you want to play.

Note: You can find videos in your Videos library and sounds in your Music library. To view the files in your libraries, see page 54.

■ The Windows Media Player window appears and the video or sound begins to play.

2 To display controls you can use to adjust the playback of the video or sound, move the mouse over the window.

■ The playback controls appear.

Note: To hide the playback controls, move the mouse away from the window.

Tip

Why does the Welcome to Windows Media Player window appear when I try to play a video or sound?

The first time Windows Media Player starts, the Welcome to Windows Media Player window appears, asking you to choose your settings for the player. In the window, click **Recommended settings** and then click **Finish**. These settings make Windows Media Player your default program for playing sound and video files, allow the program to automatically get information for your media files online and more.

Tip

Can I use the entire screen to view a video?

Yes. You can use your entire screen to view a video. While watching a video, position the mouse over the Windows Media Player window, and then click at the bottom-right corner of the window. The video will continue playing using your entire screen. To once again view the video in a window, click at the bottom-right corner of your screen.

3 To adjust the volume, drag the slider ( ) left or right to decrease or increase the volume.

Note: If the slider does not appear, increase the size of the window to display the slider. To resize a window, see page 21.

4 To turn off the sound, click (changes to).

■ You can click to once again turn on the sound.

5 To pause or stop playing the video or sound, click Stop ( ) or Pause ( ). changes to .

■ You can click to once again play the video or sound.

■ This bar indicates the progress of the video or sound.

6 When you finish playing the video or sound, click to close the Windows Media Player window.

PLAY A MUSIC CD

When playing a music CD, you can pause or stop the play of the CD at any time. You can also choose to play the previous or next song on the CD.

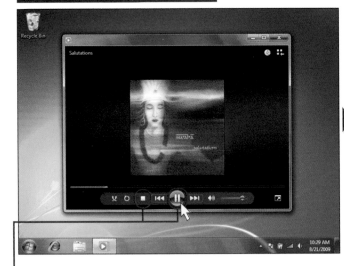

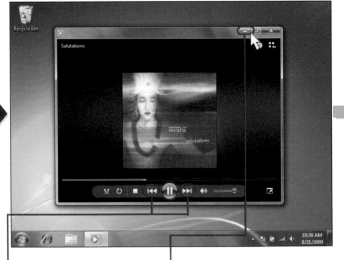

PAUSE OR STOP PLAY

1 To pause or stop playing the CD, click Stop (☐) or Pause (⏸). ⏸ changes to ▶.

■ To once again play the CD, click ▶.

PLAY ANOTHER SONG

1 Click ⏮ or ⏭ to play the previous or next song on the CD.

MINIMIZE THE WINDOW

1 If you want to perform other tasks on your computer while playing the CD, you can click ▬ to minimize the Windows Media Player window.

■ The window disappears from your screen.

Tip

Can I play the songs on a music CD in random order?

Yes. If you want to play the songs on a music CD in random order, click ⚡ at the bottom of the Windows Media Player window. The songs will now play in random order. To once again play the songs in order, click ⚡ again. If ⚡ does not appear at the bottom of the window, increase the size of the window. To resize a window, see page 21.

Tip

Can I have a music CD play again automatically?

Yes. If you want a music CD to automatically start playing again after every song has played once, click 🔄 at the bottom of the Windows Media Player window. The music CD will now play again automatically. To stop the CD from repeating, click 🔄 again. If 🔄 does not appear at the bottom of the window, increase the size of the window. To resize a window, see page 21.

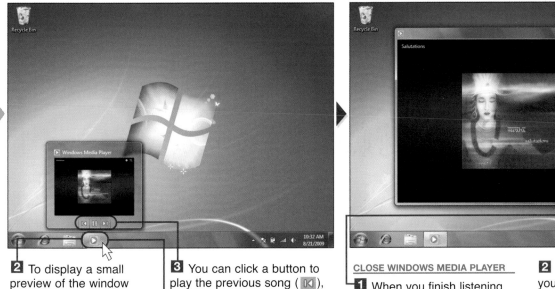

2 To display a small preview of the window at any time, move the mouse ⟍ over ▶ on the taskbar. A small preview of the window appears.

3 You can click a button to play the previous song (◀◀), play the next song (▶▶) or pause the play of the CD (❚❚).

4 To redisplay the Windows Media Player window at any time, click ▶ on the taskbar.

CLOSE WINDOWS MEDIA PLAYER

1 When you finish listening to the CD, click ✖ to close the Windows Media Player window.

2 Remove the CD from your drive.

CREATE A PLAYLIST

You can create personalized lists, called playlists, of your favorite songs, videos and pictures.

Playlists allow you to group items you would like to listen to or view regularly. For example, you can create a playlist that contains your favorite rock songs.

The first time Windows Media Player starts, the Welcome to Windows Media Player window appears, asking you to choose your settings for the player. See the top of page 109 for information on choosing your settings.

CREATE A PLAYLIST

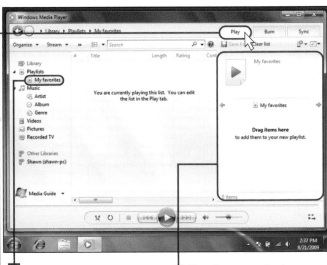

1 Click ▶ to start Windows Media Player.

■ The Windows Media Player window appears.

2 Click **Create playlist** to create a new playlist.

3 Type a name for the new playlist and then press the Enter key.

4 To add an item to the playlist, such as a song, picture or video, double-click the playlist.

5 Click the **Play** tab to display the list pane.

■ The list pane displays an area where you can add items to the playlist. The name of the playlist appears at the top of the list pane.

How do I change the order of items in a playlist?

To change the order of items in a playlist, double-click the name of the playlist you want to change in the Windows Media Player window. In the list pane, drag an item up or down in the playlist. When you finish making your changes, click **Save list**.

How do I add or remove items from a playlist?

To add or remove items from a playlist, double-click the name of the playlist you want to change in the Windows Media Player window. To add another item, locate the item and then drag it to the list pane. To remove an item, click the item in the list pane and then press the Delete key. When you finish making your changes, click **Save list**.

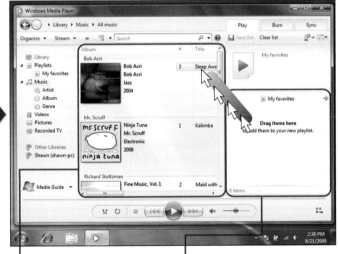

6 Locate an item you want to add to your playlist.

Note: For information on how to find items in Windows Media Player, see page 114.

7 Position the mouse over the item and then drag the item to the list pane.

Note: To add more than one item at once, press and hold down the Ctrl key as you click each item you want to add. Then drag the items to the list pane.

■ The item appears in the list pane.

8 Repeat steps **6** and **7** for each item you want to add to the playlist.

9 When you finish adding items to the playlist, click **Save list** to save all the items you added.

10 To play all the items in a playlist, double-click the name of the playlist.

COPY SONGS FROM A MUSIC CD

You can copy songs from a music CD onto your computer.

Copying songs from a music CD, also known as "ripping" music, allows you to play the songs at any time without having to insert the CD into your computer. Copying songs from a music CD also allows you to later copy the songs to a recordable CD or a portable device, such as an MP3 player.

The first time Windows Media Player starts, the Welcome to Windows Media Player window appears, asking you to choose your settings for the player. See the top of page 109 for information on choosing your settings.

COPY SONGS FROM A MUSIC CD

1 Insert a music CD into your computer's CD drive.

■ The Windows Media Player window appears and the CD begins to play.

2 Position the mouse over the window and then click ⊞ to display the Windows Media Player Library.

Note: If the Windows Media Player Library already appears, you do not need to perform step 2.

■ The Windows Media Player Library appears.

■ This area displays information about each song on the CD.

Note: For information on how Windows Media Player obtains information about the CD, such as the name of each song, see the top of page 111.

Tip

How can I play a song I copied from a music CD?

Songs you copy from a music CD appear in the Windows Media Player Library. To find and play songs in the Windows Media Player Library, see page 114. Songs you copy from a music CD also appear in the Music library on your computer. The Music library displays a folder for each artist whose songs you have copied to your computer. To view the Music library, see page 54. When you see a song you want to play in the Music library, double-click the song to play it.

■ Windows Media Player will copy each song that displays a check mark.

3 To add (✔) or remove ( ) a check mark for a song, click the box ( ) beside the song.

4 Click **Rip CD** to start copying the songs you selected to your computer.

*Note: You may need to click » at the top of the window to see the **Rip CD** option.*

■ This column indicates the status of the copy.

■ To stop the copy at any time, click **Stop rip**.

5 When you finish copying songs from the music CD, click to close the Windows Media Player window.

COPY SONGS TO A CD

You can use Windows Media Player to copy songs on your computer to a CD. Copying songs to a CD is known as "burning" a CD.

The first time Windows Media Player starts, the Welcome to Windows Media Player window appears, asking you to choose your settings for the player. See the top of page 109 for information on choosing your settings.

COPY SONGS TO A CD

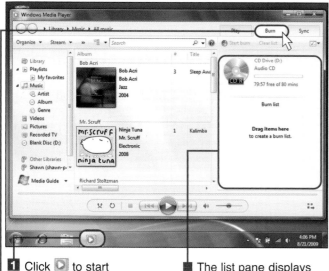

1 Click ▶ to start Windows Media Player.

■ The Windows Media Player window appears.

2 Click the **Burn** tab.

■ The list pane displays an area where you can add the songs you want to copy to a CD.

3 Insert a blank, recordable CD into your recordable CD drive.

4 Locate a song you want to copy to the CD.

Note: For information on how to find songs in Windows Media Player, see page 114.

5 Position the mouse ▷ over the song and then drag the song to the list pane.

Note: To add more than one song at once, press and hold down the Ctrl *key as you click each song you want to add. Then drag the songs to the list pane.*

Tip

Is there a faster way to select the songs I want to copy?

Yes. If you want to add all the songs in a playlist or on an album to a CD, drag the playlist or album cover to the list pane. For information on playlists, see page 116.

Tip

How do I change the songs I selected to copy?

If you want to change the order of the songs you selected to copy to a CD, drag a song up or down in the list.

If you want to remove a song you selected to copy to a CD, click the song in the list and then press the `Delete` key. Removing a song from the list does not delete the song from the Windows Media Player Library or from your computer.

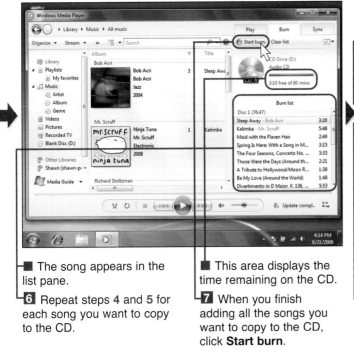

■ The song appears in the list pane.

6 Repeat steps **4** and **5** for each song you want to copy to the CD.

■ This area displays the time remaining on the CD.

7 When you finish adding all the songs you want to copy to the CD, click **Start burn**.

■ This area shows the progress of the copy.

■ To cancel the copy at any time, click **Cancel burn**.

■ When the copy is complete, Windows automatically ejects the CD from your CD drive.

8 Click ✕ to close the Windows Media Player window.

COPY SONGS TO A PORTABLE DEVICE

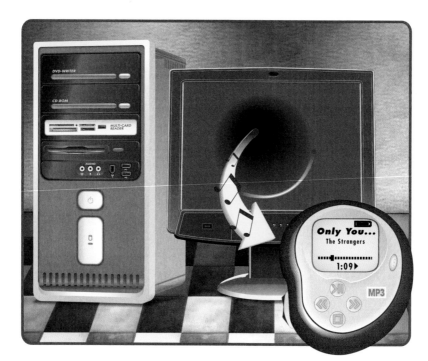

You can use Windows Media Player to copy music, pictures and videos on your computer to a portable device, such as an MP3 player.

Copying items to a portable device is known as "synchronizing" or "syncing."

The first time Windows Media Player starts, the Welcome to Windows Media Player window appears, asking you to choose your settings for the player. See the top of page 109 for information on choosing your settings.

SET UP A PORTABLE DEVICE

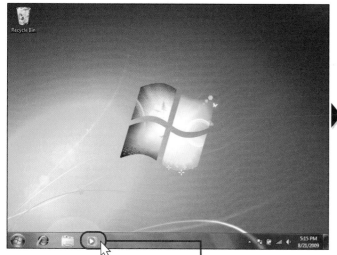

1 Turn on your portable device and then connect the device to your computer.

Note: If the AutoPlay window appears, click [X] to close the window.

2 Click [▶] to start Windows Media Player.

■ The Windows Media Player window appears.

■ The first time you connect a portable device to your computer, the Device Setup wizard appears.

*Note: If the wizard does not appear, click the **Sync** tab, click [☑▾] below the tab, and then click **Set up sync** to display the wizard.*

■ This area describes how you will copy songs and other items from Windows Media Player to your portable device. The wizard selects the best method for your device.

3 Click **Finish**.

Tip

Why can't my portable device update automatically?

If your portable device's storage capacity is more than 4 GB and your entire Windows Media Player Library can fit on the device, Windows Media Player will be set up to automatically update your portable device. If your portable device's storage capacity is less than 4 GB or your entire Windows Media Player Library cannot fit on the device, you will need to manually copy songs and other items to your portable device.

 Tip

How can I safely remove a portable device from my computer?

If you want to safely remove a portable device from your computer, click the Safely Remove Hardware and Eject Media icon ( ) at the bottom-right corner of your screen. On the list of devices that appears, click the portable device you want to safely remove. A message will appear, indicating that you can safely remove the device.

Note: If you do not see the icon at the bottom-right corner of your screen, click ▲ to display the icon.

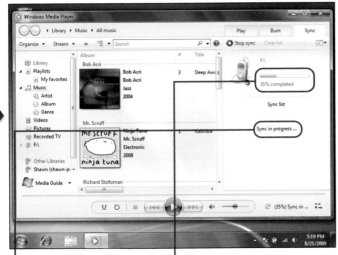

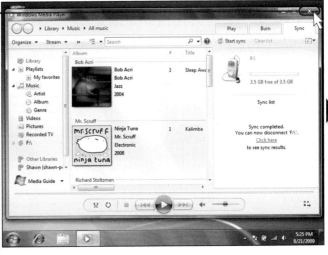

■ If Windows Media Player can update your portable device automatically, it will immediately copy your entire Windows Media Player Library to your portable device.

Note: If Windows Media Player cannot update your portable device automatically, see page 124 to manually add songs and other items to your device.

■ This area shows the progress of the copy.

■ When the copy is complete, you can disconnect the portable device from your computer.

4 Click to close the Windows Media Player window.

■ From now on, every time you connect your portable device to your computer when Windows Media Player is open, your device will be updated automatically to match the contents of Windows Media Player.

 CONTINUED

COPY SONGS TO A PORTABLE DEVICE

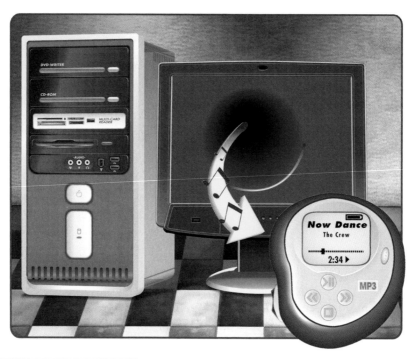

Windows Media Player may need you to create a list of the songs, pictures and videos that you want to copy to your portable device.

You will need to create a list of the items you want to copy to your portable device if your device's storage capacity is less than 4 GB or your entire Windows Media Player Library cannot fit on the device.

MANUALLY UPDATE A PORTABLE DEVICE

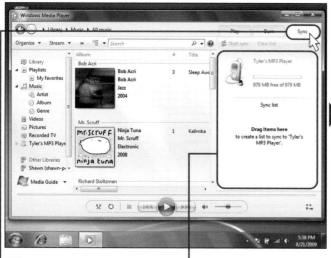

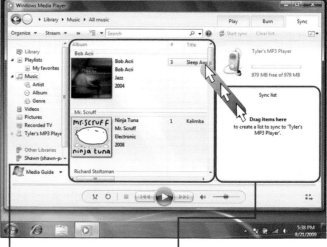

1 To manually copy songs and other items to your portable device, perform steps **1** to **3** on page 122.

2 Click the **Sync** tab.

■ The list pane displays an area where you can add the songs, pictures and videos that you want to copy to your portable device.

3 Locate a song, picture or video that you want to copy to the portable device.

Note: For information on how to find items in Windows Media Player, see page 114.

4 Position the mouse ⬚ over the song, picture or video and then drag the item to the list pane.

Note: To add more than one item at once, press and hold down the Ctrl *key as you click each item you want to add. Then drag the items to the list pane.*

Tip

Is there a faster way to select the songs I want to copy?

Yes. If you want to add all the songs in a playlist or on an album to a portable device, drag the playlist or album cover to the list pane. For information on playlists, see page 116.

 Tip

How do I change the songs I selected to copy?

If you want to change the order of the songs, pictures or videos you selected to copy to your portable device, drag an item up or down in the list.

If you want to remove a song, picture or video you selected to copy to your portable device, click the item in the list and then press the Delete key. Removing an item from the list does not delete the item from the Windows Media Player Library or from your computer.

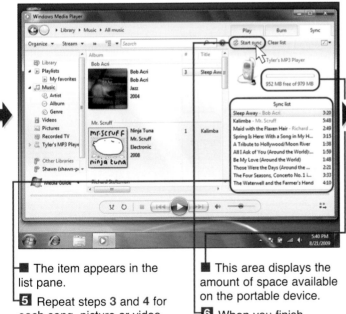

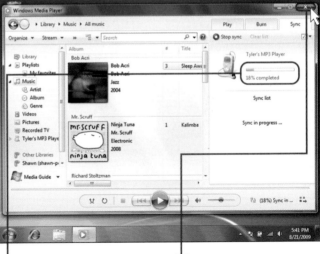

■ The item appears in the list pane.

5 Repeat steps **3** and **4** for each song, picture or video that you want to copy to the portable device.

■ This area displays the amount of space available on the portable device.

6 When you finish adding all the items that you want to copy to the portable device, click **Start sync**.

■ This area shows the progress of the copy.

■ When the copy is complete, you can disconnect the portable device from your computer.

7 Click [X] to close the Windows Media Player window.

PLAY A DVD MOVIE

You can use Windows Media Player to play DVD movies on your computer.

If you have a laptop computer, using your computer to play DVD movies can be especially useful when traveling.

The first time Windows Media Player starts, the Welcome to Windows Media Player window appears, asking you to choose your settings for the player. See the top of page 109 for information on choosing your settings.

PLAY A DVD MOVIE

Note: To hide the playback controls, move the mouse ☐ away from the bottom of your screen.

1 Insert the DVD movie you want to play into your computer's DVD drive.

■ The DVD movie begins playing, typically filling your entire screen.

■ After a few moments, the DVD's main menu usually appears, displaying options you can select, such as an option to play the movie or select a specific scene. To select an option, click the option.

2 To display controls you can use to adjust the playback of the movie, move your mouse.

■ The playback controls appear.

3 To skip to the previous or next chapter of the movie, click ◄◄ or ►►.

Tip

Why can't I play a DVD movie?

Before you can play DVD movies, your computer must have a DVD drive and a compatible DVD decoder installed. A DVD decoder is software that allows your computer to play DVD movies. If you see a message indicating that you are missing a DVD decoder, you will need to obtain a decoder in order to play DVD movies on your computer.

Tip

Do I have to use the entire screen to watch a DVD movie?

No. You can play a DVD movie within a window so you can perform other tasks on your computer while the movie plays. To view a movie in a window at any time, click ▼ at the bottom-right corner of your screen. Your movie will continue playing in a window. To once again view the movie using the full screen, position the mouse ⌖ over the window and then click ◩ at the bottom-right corner of the window.

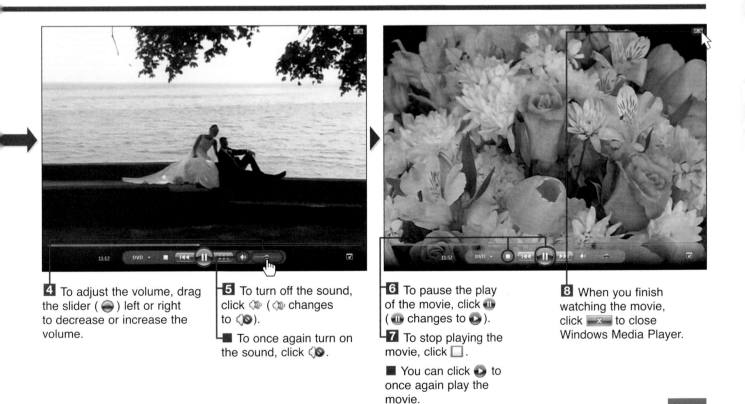

4 To adjust the volume, drag the slider (⬤) left or right to decrease or increase the volume.

5 To turn off the sound, click ◁》 (◁》 changes to ◁⊘).

■ To once again turn on the sound, click ◁⊘ .

6 To pause the play of the movie, click ❚❚ (❚❚ changes to ▶).

7 To stop playing the movie, click ☐ .

■ You can click ▶ to once again play the movie.

8 When you finish watching the movie, click ✕ to close Windows Media Player.

TRANSFER VIDEO FROM A VIDEO CAMERA

You can easily transfer video on a video camera to your computer.

You can use Windows Live Photo Gallery to transfer video on a video camera to your computer. Windows Live Photo Gallery is not included in Windows 7, but the program is available for free at the Windows Live Essentials website (http://download.live.com). For more information on this website, see page 50.

TRANSFER VIDEO FROM A VIDEO CAMERA

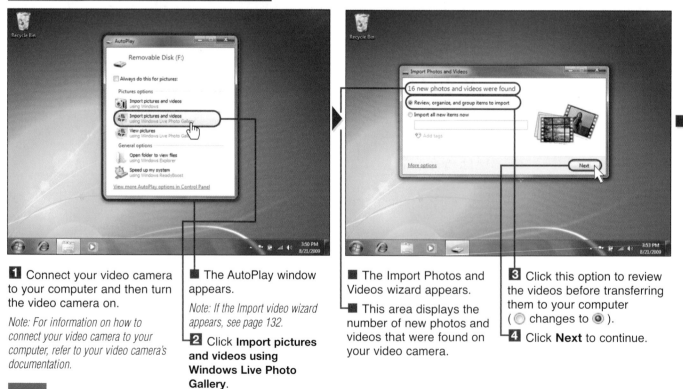

1 Connect your video camera to your computer and then turn the video camera on.

Note: For information on how to connect your video camera to your computer, refer to your video camera's documentation.

■ The AutoPlay window appears.

Note: If the Import video wizard appears, see page 132.

2 Click **Import pictures and videos using Windows Live Photo Gallery**.

■ The Import Photos and Videos wizard appears.

■ This area displays the number of new photos and videos that were found on your video camera.

3 Click this option to review the videos before transferring them to your computer (◯ changes to ◉).

4 Click **Next** to continue.

Tip

How can I transfer all the new video on my video camera to my computer?

If you want to transfer all the new video on your video camera to your computer, perform steps **1** and **2** below and then click **Import all new items now**. Then click the empty box in the wizard and type a name for the video. To add one or more tags to the video to help you later find the video, click **Add tags**. Then type one or more tags, separated by semicolons (;), and then press the Enter key. Click **Import** to transfer the video to your computer.

Note: Windows will use the name you type to name the new folder on your computer that will store the video. For information on tags, see page 130.

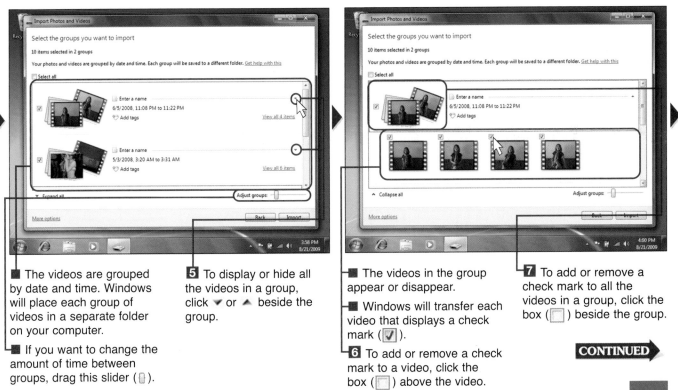

■ The videos are grouped by date and time. Windows will place each group of videos in a separate folder on your computer.

■ If you want to change the amount of time between groups, drag this slider ( ).

5 To display or hide all the videos in a group, click ▼ or ▲ beside the group.

■ The videos in the group appear or disappear.

■ Windows will transfer each video that displays a check mark (✓).

6 To add or remove a check mark to a video, click the box ( ) above the video.

7 To add or remove a check mark to all the videos in a group, click the box ( ) beside the group.

CONTINUED

TRANSFER VIDEO FROM A VIDEO CAMERA

When you transfer video to your computer, you can specify a name for the video and add tags to the video.

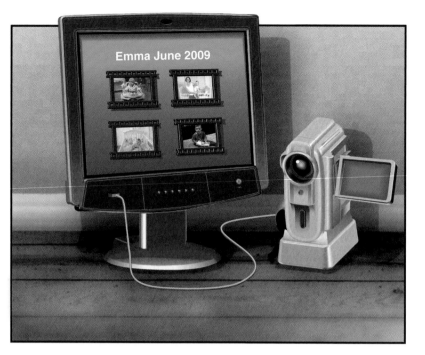

Windows will use the name you specify to name the new folder on your computer that will store the video.

A tag is a meaningful word or phrase that you can add to videos to help you find and organize your videos. For example, you can use a tag to describe the location, people or event shown in your videos.

TRANSFER VIDEO FROM A VIDEO CAMERA (CONTINUED)

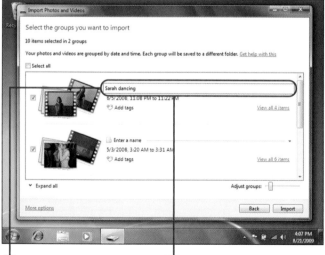

8 To enter a name for a group of videos you selected to transfer to your computer, click **Enter a name** beside the group.

9 Type a name for the group and then press the Enter key.

10 To add one or more tags to a group of videos to help you later find the videos, click **Add tags** beside the group.

11 Type one or more tags, separated by semicolons (;), and then press the Enter key.

12 Click **Import** to transfer the video to your computer.

Tip

How do I play a video in Windows Live Photo Gallery?

After you transfer video from a video camera to your computer, you can play the video in Windows Live Photo Gallery. To do so, double-click the video you want to play. When you finish watching the video, click **Back to gallery** to return to the photo and video gallery.

Tip

How can I change where videos are placed on my computer?

When you transfer video to your computer, Windows may place the video in the My Pictures folder. If you want to place the video in the My Videos folder, click **More options** in the Import Photos and Videos wizard when transferring video to your computer. In the dialog box that appears, click the area beside Import to and then click **My Videos**. Then click **OK**.

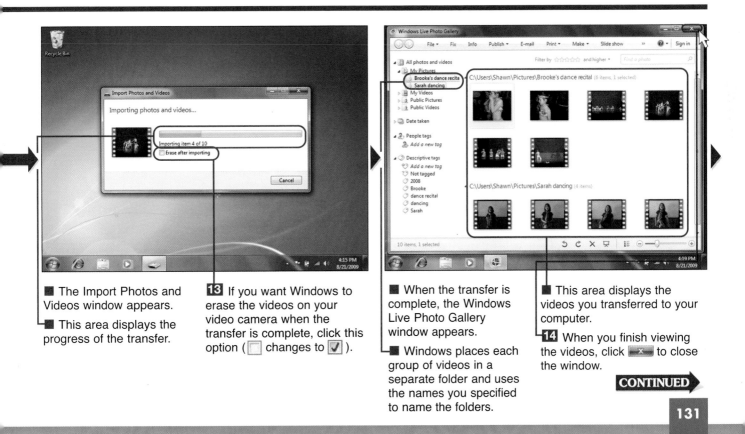

■ The Import Photos and Videos window appears.

■ This area displays the progress of the transfer.

13 If you want Windows to erase the videos on your video camera when the transfer is complete, click this option (☐ changes to ☑).

■ When the transfer is complete, the Windows Live Photo Gallery window appears.

■ Windows places each group of videos in a separate folder and uses the names you specified to name the folders.

■ This area displays the videos you transferred to your computer.

14 When you finish viewing the videos, click ✕ to close the window.

CONTINUED ▶

TRANSFER VIDEO FROM A VIDEO CAMERA

If you have a video camera that stores video on a videotape, you can easily transfer video you recorded to your computer.

TRANSFER VIDEO STORED ON A VIDEOTAPE

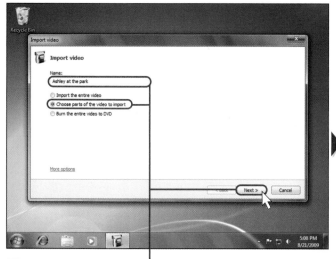

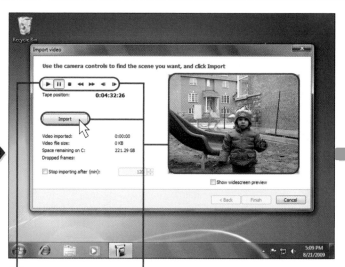

1 Connect your video camera to your computer, turn the video camera on and set it to the mode that plays back video.

■ The Import video wizard appears.

2 Type a name for your video.

3 Click this option to choose the parts of the videotape that you want to transfer (○ changes to ◉).

4 Click **Next** to continue.

5 To find the point in the video where you want to start transferring video, use these controls or the controls on your video camera.

■ You can play (▶), pause (‖), stop (■), rewind (◀◀), fast forward (▶▶) and move to the previous or next frame (◀‖, ‖▶).

■ This area displays the video.

6 When you are ready to transfer the video to your computer, click **Import**.

Tip

How can I transfer my entire videotape to my computer?

If you want to transfer your entire videotape to your computer, perform steps **1** and **2** below and then click **Import the entire video**. Click **Next** to start transferring all the video on the videotape to your computer.

Import video

Import video

Name:
Andrew's first year

○ Import the entire video
○ Choose parts of the video to import
○ Burn the entire video to DVD

More options

< Back   Next >   Cancel

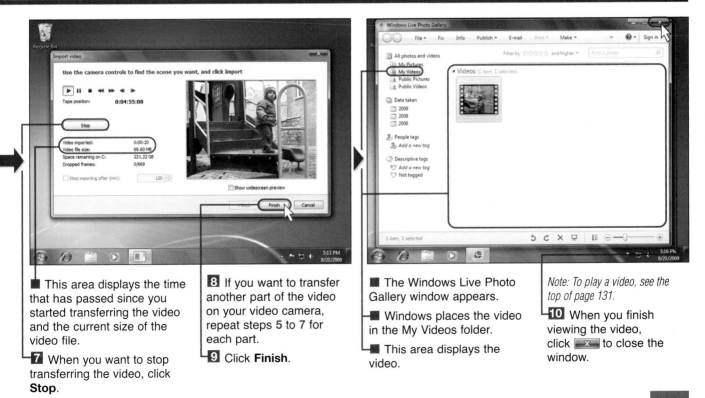

■ This area displays the time that has passed since you started transferring the video and the current size of the video file.

7 When you want to stop transferring the video, click **Stop**.

8 If you want to transfer another part of the video on your video camera, repeat steps **5** to **7** for each part.

9 Click **Finish**.

■ The Windows Live Photo Gallery window appears.

■ Windows places the video in the My Videos folder.

■ This area displays the video.

Note: To play a video, see the top of page 131.

10 When you finish viewing the video, click ✕ to close the window.

Create Movies

You can use Windows Live Movie Maker to create movies and slide shows from your favorite videos and photos on your computer. You can then share the movies with your family, friends or the whole world.

Windows Live Movie Maker is not included in Windows 7, but the program is available for free at the Windows Live Essentials website (http://download.live.com). For more information on this website, see page 50.

START WINDOWS LIVE MOVIE MAKER

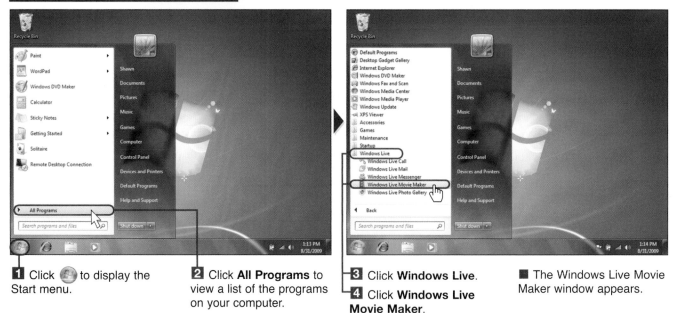

1 Click ![icon] to display the Start menu.

2 Click **All Programs** to view a list of the programs on your computer.

3 Click **Windows Live**.

4 Click **Windows Live Movie Maker**.

■ The Windows Live Movie Maker window appears.

ADD VIDEOS AND PHOTOS

Adding the videos and photos you want to include in your movie is the first step in making a movie.

ADD VIDEOS AND PHOTOS

1 Click the **Home** tab.

2 To add a video or photo to your movie, click **Add videos and photos**.

■ The Add Videos and Photos dialog box appears.

■ This area lists commonly used locations on your computer. You can click a location to display the files in the location.

3 Locate the video or photo you want to add to your movie.

4 Click the video or photo.

Note: To add more than one video or photo, press and hold down the `Ctrl` *key as you click each video or photo.*

5 Click **Open**.

CONTINUED

137

ADD VIDEOS AND PHOTOS

After adding videos and photos to your movie, you can change the order of the videos and photos. You can also watch a preview of your movie.

ADD VIDEOS AND PHOTOS (CONTINUED)

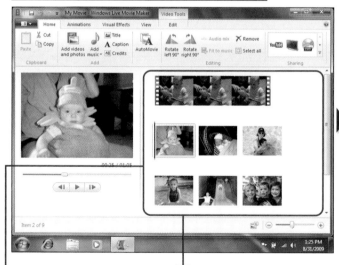

■ The video or photo you selected appears on the storyboard.

■ The storyboard shows the order in which the videos and photos you add will play in your movie.

6 To add another video or photo to your movie, repeat steps **2** to **5** on page 137 for each video or photo you want to add.

REORDER VIDEOS AND PHOTOS

1 To change the location of a video or photo in your movie, position the mouse over a video or photo you want to move.

2 Drag the video or photo to a new location on the storyboard.

■ As you drag, a gray vertical line indicates where the video or photo will appear.

Tip

How do I remove a video or photo from my movie?

To remove a video or photo you no longer want to appear in your movie, click the video or photo on the storyboard, and then press the Delete key. The video or photo disappears from the storyboard but will remain on your computer.

Tip

How can I quickly create a movie?

You can use the AutoMovie feature to quickly create a professional-looking movie. This feature will automatically add a title, credits, transitions and pan and zoom effects to your movie, as well as make your movie, and any music you add, end at the same time.

After you finish adding the videos, photos and music you want your movie to include, click the **Home** tab and then click **AutoMovie**. In the dialog box that appears, click **OK**. When AutoMovie is done, click **Close**.

Note: To add music to a movie, see page 146. To add a title, credits, transitions and pan and zoom effects to a movie yourself, see pages 140 to 144.

PREVIEW A MOVIE

■1 To preview your entire movie, click the left side of the first item on the storyboard.

Note: To preview only part of your movie, click the location on the storyboard where you want to start the preview.

■ A black vertical line on the storyboard indicates the current location in the movie.

■2 Click ► to preview the movie.

■ The movie will begin playing on the preview monitor.

■ This area displays the elapsed time and the total time of your movie.

■3 To fast forward or rewind the movie, drag the slider (○) forward or backward.

■4 To pause the movie, click ‖ (‖ changes to ►).

■5 To display the previous or next frame in the movie, click ◄‖ or ‖► .

ADD TRANSITIONS, PAN AND ZOOM EFFECTS

You can add transitions to your movie to customize the way your movie moves from one video or photo to the next. For example, you can have a video fade out as the following video fades in.

You can also add pan and zoom effects to photos in your movie.

A pan effect moves across a photo. For example, you may want to pan across the photo of a city skyline.

A zoom effect zooms in or out of a photo. For example, you may want to zoom in on a person's face.

ADD A TRANSITION

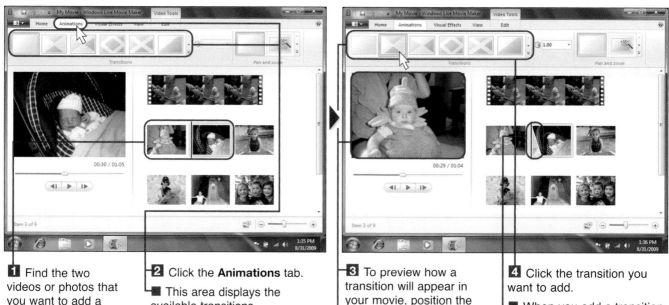

1 Find the two videos or photos that you want to add a transition between. Then click the second video or photo.

2 Click the **Animations** tab.

■ This area displays the available transitions.

Note: To browse through the available transitions, click ▲ and ▼ . If you want to view the available transitions in a larger area, click ▼ .

3 To preview how a transition will appear in your movie, position the mouse ⓘ over a transition.

■ A preview of the transition appears in the preview monitor.

4 Click the transition you want to add.

■ When you add a transition to a video or photo, a gray area appears on the left side of the video or photo.

Tip

Can I add the same transition, pan or zoom effect to many videos and photos at once?

To add the same transition to many videos and photos at once, press and hold the `Ctrl` key as you click each video and photo. Then click the transition you want to add to each video and photo.

To add the same pan or zoom effect to many photos at once, press and hold the `Ctrl` key as you click each photo. Then click the pan or zoom effect that you want to add to each photo.

Note: To quickly select all the videos and photos in your movie, click a blank area on the storyboard and then press and hold the `Ctrl` key as you press the `A` key.

 Tip

How do I remove a transition, pan or zoom effect from my movie?

To remove a transition that appears between two videos or photos, click the second video or photo and then click the **Animations** tab. Then click the first transition option (▢).

To remove a pan or zoom effect from a photo, click the photo and then click the **Animations** tab. Then click the first pan and zoom effect option (▢).

ADD A PAN OR ZOOM EFFECT

1 Click the photo you want to add a pan or zoom effect to.

2 Click the **Animations** tab.

■ This area displays the available pan and zoom effects.

Note: To browse through the available pan and zoom effects, click ▲ and ▼. If you want to view the available pan and zoom effects in a larger area, click ▼.

3 To preview how a pan or zoom effect will appear in your movie, position the mouse ▷ over an effect.

■ A preview of the pan or zoom effect appears in the preview monitor.

4 Click the pan or zoom effect you want to add.

■ When you add a pan or zoom effect to a photo, a symbol (⊞) appears at the top-left corner of the photo.

ADD VISUAL EFFECTS AND TRIM VIDEOS

You can add a visual effect to your movie to give a video or photo a certain appearance. For example, you can have a video or photo appear in black and white.

You can also trim a video to hide parts of the video you do not want to play in your movie. You can trim the beginning of a video, the end of a video, or both.

When you add a visual effect or trim a video in your movie, the original video or photo on your computer will not be affected.

ADD A VISUAL EFFECT

1 Click the video or photo you want to add a visual effect to.

2 Click the **Visual Effects** tab.

■ This area displays the available visual effects.

Note: To browse through the available visual effects, click ▲ and ▼. If you want to view the available visual effects in a larger area, click ▼.

3 To preview how a visual effect will appear in your movie, position the mouse over a visual effect.

■ A preview of the visual effect appears in the preview monitor.

4 Click the visual effect you want to add.

■ When you add a visual effect to a video or photo, a symbol (⊞) appears at the top-left corner of the video or photo.

Tip

How do I remove a visual effect from my movie?

To remove a visual effect from a video or photo, click the video or photo and then click the **Visual Effects** tab. Then click the first visual effect option ( ).

Tip

After I trim a video, can I undo the changes I made?

Yes. If you trimmed too much or too little of a video or decide you no longer want to trim a video, you can undo the changes you made. To do so, perform steps **1** to **3** below, and then drag the handles ( ) to the locations where you want the video to begin and stop playing. Click **Save trim** to save your changes.

TRIM A VIDEO

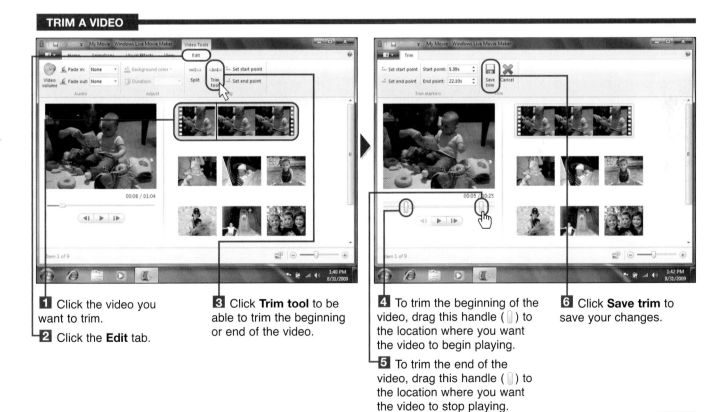

1 Click the video you want to trim.

2 Click the **Edit** tab.

3 Click **Trim tool** to be able to trim the beginning or end of the video.

4 To trim the beginning of the video, drag this handle ( ) to the location where you want the video to begin playing.

5 To trim the end of the video, drag this handle ( ) to the location where you want the video to stop playing.

6 Click **Save trim** to save your changes.

You can add a title at the beginning of your movie to help introduce your movie.

You may also want to add a title in the middle of your movie to help introduce a new section in your movie.

When you add a title to your movie, you can select an effect for the title. For example, you may want the text to fly in from the left or right.

ADD A TITLE

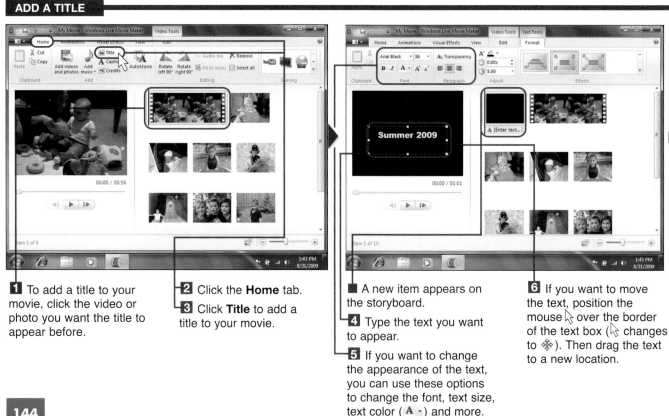

1 To add a title to your movie, click the video or photo you want the title to appear before.

2 Click the **Home** tab.

3 Click **Title** to add a title to your movie.

■ A new item appears on the storyboard.

4 Type the text you want to appear.

5 If you want to change the appearance of the text, you can use these options to change the font, text size, text color (**A** ▾) and more.

6 If you want to move the text, position the mouse ⬏ over the border of the text box (⬏ changes to ✥). Then drag the text to a new location.

Tip

How do I make changes to a title I added to my movie?

If you later want to make changes to a title in your movie, click the title on the storyboard. Click the **Format** tab, and then make the changes you want to the title. For example, you may want to select a different background color or text effect for the title.

If you want to remove a title you added to a movie, click the title and then press the Delete key.

Tip

Can I add captions and credits to a movie?

Yes. You can add a caption to add your own words, such as a person's name, to a photo or video in your movie. You can also add credits at the end of your movie.

✓ To add a caption, click the video or photo you want to add text to. Click the **Home** tab and then click **Caption**. Type the text you want to appear on the video or photo.

✓ To add credits, click the **Home** tab and then click **Credits**. A new item appears at the end of the storyboard. Type the text you want to appear in the credits.

SELECT A BACKGROUND COLOR

1 Click ▼ beside 🎨 to display the available background colors.

2 Click the background color you want to use.

Note: If the text disappears, click the preview monitor to once again display the text.

SELECT A TEXT EFFECT

■ This area displays the available text effects.

Note: To browse through the available effects, click ▼ and ▲ . If you want to view the available effects in a larger area, click ▼ .

1 To preview how an effect will appear in your movie, position the mouse ⌖ over an effect.

■ A preview of the effect appears in the preview monitor.

2 Click the effect you want to add.

Customize Windows

You can change the picture used to decorate your desktop.

Windows comes with many desktop backgrounds that you can choose from. You can also use one of your own pictures as your desktop background.

You can also change your desktop background by selecting a different theme. To select a different theme, see page 158.

CHANGE THE DESKTOP BACKGROUND

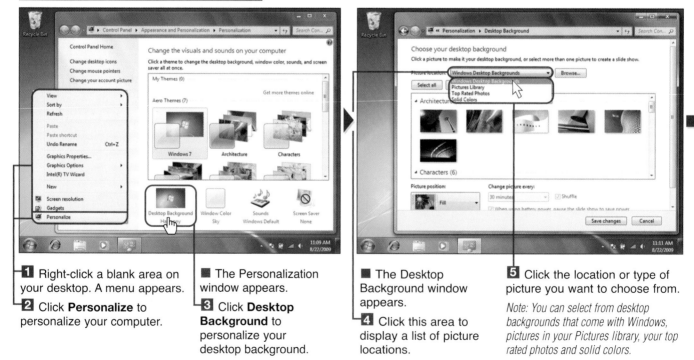

1 Right-click a blank area on your desktop. A menu appears.

2 Click **Personalize** to personalize your computer.

■ The Personalization window appears.

3 Click **Desktop Background** to personalize your desktop background.

■ The Desktop Background window appears.

4 Click this area to display a list of picture locations.

5 Click the location or type of picture you want to choose from.

Note: You can select from desktop backgrounds that come with Windows, pictures in your Pictures library, your top rated photos and solid colors.

Tip

Can I create a desktop slideshow?

Yes. You can have Windows automatically change the desktop background every day, every hour or after a time period you select. In the Desktop Background window, click the top-left corner of each picture you want to include in the slide show (☐ changes to ☑). If you want to quickly select all the pictures, click **Select all**. To specify how often you want the desktop picture to change, click the area below **Change picture every:** and select a time.

Tip

I cannot find the picture I want to use as my desktop background. What can I do?

If you cannot find the picture you want to use as your desktop background, click **Browse** in the Desktop Background window to locate the folder that contains the picture you want to use. In the dialog box that appears, click the folder that contains the picture and then click **OK**. The pictures in the folder you selected will appear in the Desktop Background window.

■ This area displays the pictures in the location you selected.

6 Click the picture you want to display on your desktop.

■ The picture you selected immediately appears on your desktop.

7 Click this area to select the way you want to position the picture on your desktop.

8 Click an option to crop the picture to fill the screen, resize the picture to fit the screen, stretch the picture to fill the screen, tile the picture to fill the screen or center the picture on the screen.

9 Click **Save changes** to save your changes.

A screen saver is a picture or animation that appears on the screen when you do not use your computer for a period of time.

You can use a screen saver to hide your work while you are away from your computer. Windows is initially set up to not display a screen saver.

CHANGE THE SCREEN SAVER

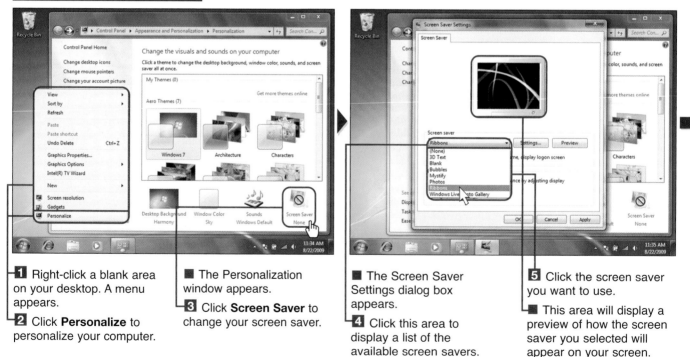

1 Right-click a blank area on your desktop. A menu appears.

2 Click **Personalize** to personalize your computer.

■ The Personalization window appears.

3 Click **Screen Saver** to change your screen saver.

■ The Screen Saver Settings dialog box appears.

4 Click this area to display a list of the available screen savers.

5 Click the screen saver you want to use.

■ This area will display a preview of how the screen saver you selected will appear on your screen.

Tip

What does the Photos screen saver do?

You can select the Photos screen saver to have the pictures in your Pictures library appear as your screen saver. Windows will rotate through all the pictures in the library. For information on the Pictures library, see page 55.

Tip

Can I customize my screen saver?

After you select the screen saver you want to use, you can click the **Settings** button to customize some screen savers. For example, if you select the 3D Text screen saver, you can customize the text that you want to appear on your screen, such as your company's name.

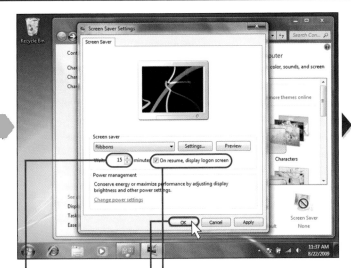

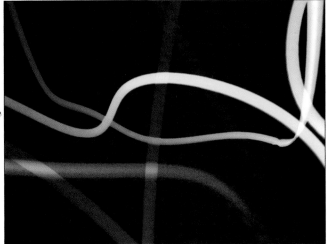

6 To specify the number of minutes your computer must be inactive before the screen saver will appear, double-click this area. Then type the number of minutes.

7 To make your computer more secure, this option requires you to log on to Windows each time you remove the screen saver. You can click this option to turn the option on (✓) or off (☐).

Note: For information on logging on to Windows, see page 185.

8 Click **OK**.

■ The screen saver appears when you do not use your computer for the number of minutes you specified.

■ You can move the mouse or press a key on the keyboard to remove the screen saver from your screen.

■ To stop a screen saver from appearing, perform steps **1** to **5**, selecting **(None)** in step **5**. Then perform step **8**.

CHANGE THE COLOR OF WINDOWS

You can add a personal touch to your computer by changing the color used to display windows on your screen. The color you select will also change the color of the taskbar and the Start menu.

You can also change the color used to display windows on your screen by selecting a different theme. To select a different theme, see page 158.

CHANGE THE COLOR OF WINDOWS

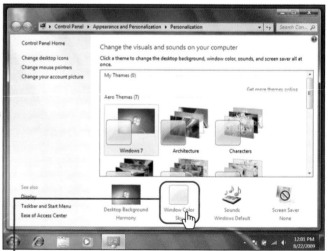

1 Right-click a blank area on your desktop. A menu appears.

2 Click **Personalize** to personalize your computer.

■ The Personalization window appears.

3 Click **Window Color** to change the color used to display windows on your screen.

■ The Window Color and Appearance window appears.

Tip

Can I create my own color?

Yes. If you do not see a color you like in the Window Color and Appearance window, click **Show color mixer** to create your own color. Drag the sliders (🔲) that appear beside Hue (color), Saturation (intensity of color) and Brightness until the windows on your screen display the color you like.

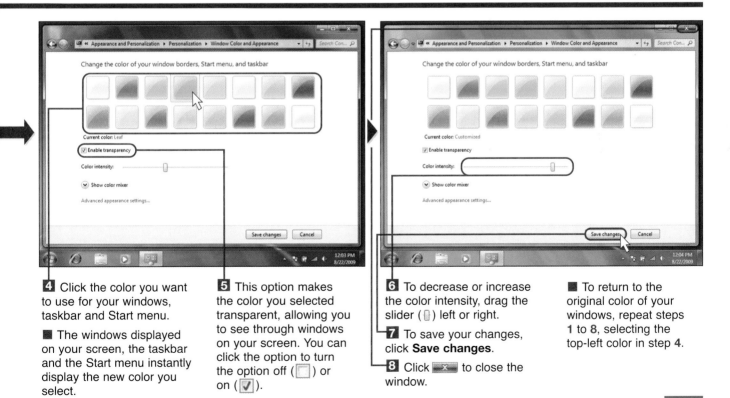

4 Click the color you want to use for your windows, taskbar and Start menu.

■ The windows displayed on your screen, the taskbar and the Start menu instantly display the new color you select.

5 This option makes the color you selected transparent, allowing you to see through windows on your screen. You can click the option to turn the option off (☐) or on (☑).

6 To decrease or increase the color intensity, drag the slider (🔲) left or right.

7 To save your changes, click **Save changes**.

8 Click ✖ to close the window.

■ To return to the original color of your windows, repeat steps 1 to 8, selecting the top-left color in step 4.

CHANGE THE THEME

You can change the
theme to personalize
the overall appearance
of Windows.

Each theme contains
several coordinated
items, including a
desktop background,
a window color,
sounds and a screen
saver. Some themes
also include unique
desktop icons and
mouse pointers.

Windows comes with
several themes that
you can choose from.

CHANGE THE THEME

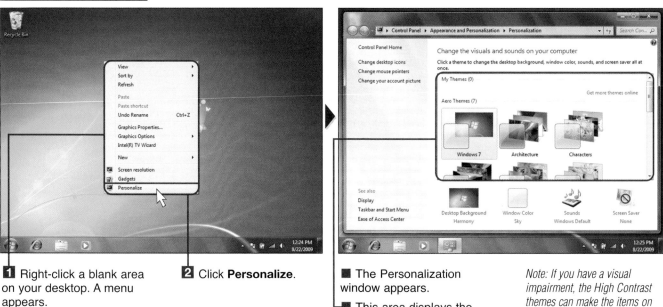

1 Right-click a blank area
on your desktop. A menu
appears.

2 Click **Personalize**.

■ The Personalization
window appears.

■ This area displays the
available themes. You can
use the scroll bar to
browse through the
available themes.

*Note: If you have a visual
impairment, the High Contrast
themes can make the items on
your screen easier to see.*

Tip

Where can I get more themes?

You can get more themes on the Internet. To quickly find more themes online, click **Get more themes online** in the Personalization window. A webpage will appear, showing a list of the available themes that you can download and use on your computer.

Tip

Can I customize a theme?

Yes. After you select a theme, you can change the parts of a theme individually by changing the desktop background, window color, sounds or screen saver. You can change one or more of these elements until the theme looks the way you want. Your customized theme will appear under My Themes in the Personalization window. For information on changing the desktop background, window color, sounds or screen saver, see pages 152, 156, 166, and 154.

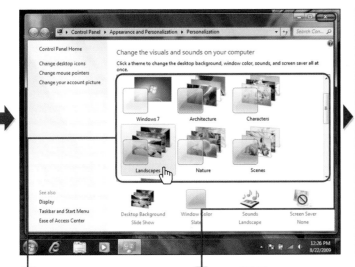

3 Click the theme you want to use.

■ Windows instantly changes your desktop background, window color, sounds and screen saver all at once to the new theme.

4 Click ▭ to close the Personalization window.

■ To return to the original theme, perform steps **1** to **4**, selecting the **Windows 7** theme in step **3**.

ADD A GADGET TO YOUR DESKTOP

You can easily add gadgets to your desktop. Gadgets are mini-programs that provide instant access to information and useful tools.

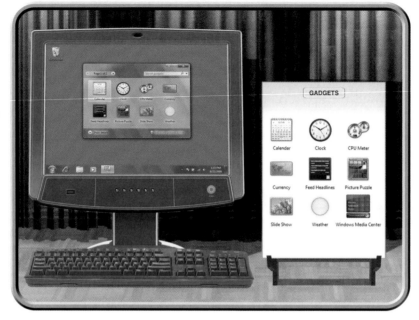

Windows comes with a variety of gadgets, including the Calendar, Clock, Feed Headlines, Slide Show and Weather gadgets.

ADD A GADGET TO YOUR DESKTOP

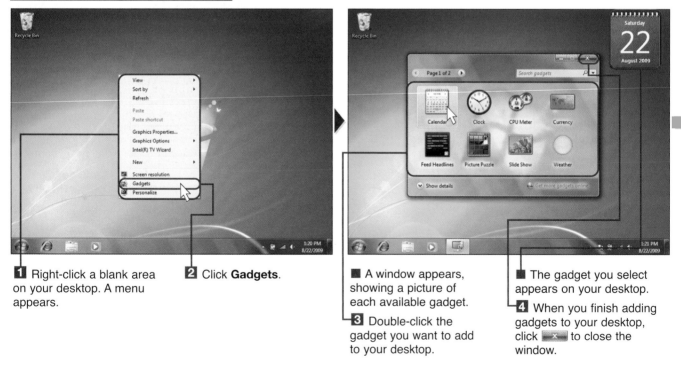

1 Right-click a blank area on your desktop. A menu appears.

2 Click **Gadgets**.

■ A window appears, showing a picture of each available gadget.

3 Double-click the gadget you want to add to your desktop.

■ The gadget you select appears on your desktop.

4 When you finish adding gadgets to your desktop, click ✕ to close the window.

Tip — **Can I customize a gadget?**

Yes. You can customize some gadgets. For example, you can choose which city's weather forecast is shown by the Weather gadget and change the style of clock used by the Clock gadget. To customize a gadget, position the mouse ⌖ over the gadget. On the toolbar that appears beside the gadget, click ⧉. Make your desired changes in the dialog box that appears and then click **OK** to save your changes.

Tip — **Where can I get more gadgets?**

You can find more gadgets on the Internet. When adding a gadget, click **Get more gadgets online** in the window showing a picture of each available gadget. A webpage appears, showing a list of the available gadgets that you can download and use on your computer. You need to install a gadget before you can display the gadget on your desktop.

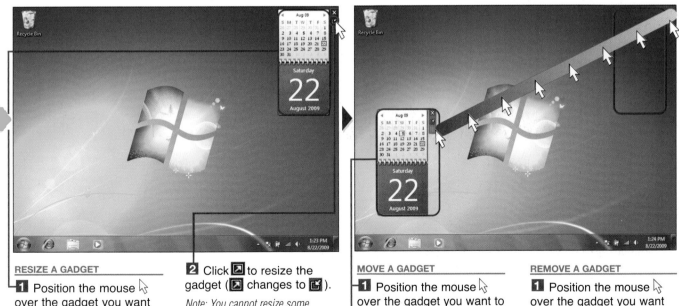

RESIZE A GADGET

1 Position the mouse ⌖ over the gadget you want to resize. A toolbar appears beside the gadget.

2 Click ⧉ to resize the gadget (⧉ changes to ⧉).

Note: You cannot resize some gadgets. To return a gadget to its original size, click ⧉.

MOVE A GADGET

1 Position the mouse ⌖ over the gadget you want to move. A toolbar appears beside the gadget.

2 Position the mouse ⌖ over ⣿ and then drag the gadget to a new location on your desktop.

REMOVE A GADGET

1 Position the mouse ⌖ over the gadget you want to remove from your desktop. A toolbar appears beside the gadget.

2 Click ✕ to remove the gadget.

You can add programs to the taskbar to provide a quick way of starting programs you regularly use.

Adding a program to the taskbar is known as "pinning" the program to the taskbar.

ADD A PROGRAM TO THE TASKBAR

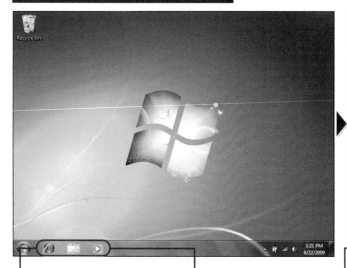

■ Windows initially displays three programs on the taskbar:

 Internet Explorer

 Windows Explorer

 Windows Media Player

■ You can start a program displayed on the taskbar by clicking the program.

■ Before you can add a program you regularly use to the taskbar, you need to find the program on the Start menu.

1 Click to display the Start menu.

2 Click **All Programs** to view a list of the programs on your computer.

Note: If the Start menu already displays the program you want to add to the taskbar, skip to step 3.

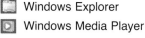

Tip

How can I quickly find a program I want to add to the taskbar?

To quickly find a program you want to add to the taskbar, click 🔵 to display the Start menu, and then click in the search box at the bottom of the Start menu. Type the name of the program you want to find. Windows will display a list of matching programs on the Start menu.

Tip

How do I remove a program from the taskbar?

If you no longer want a program to appear on the taskbar, right-click the program on the taskbar. On the menu that appears, click **Unpin this program from taskbar**. Windows will remove the program from the taskbar.

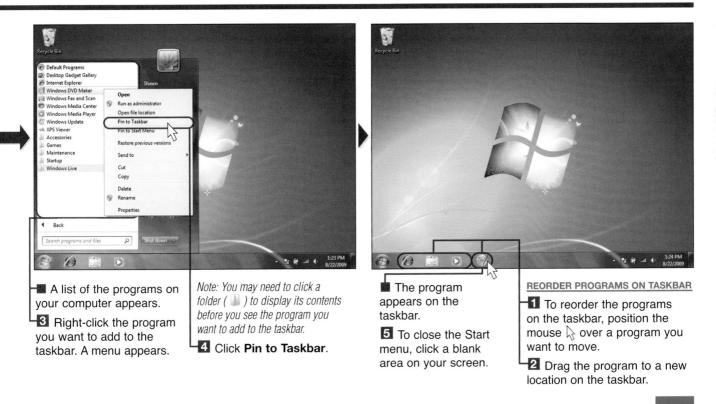

■ A list of the programs on your computer appears.

3 Right-click the program you want to add to the taskbar. A menu appears.

Note: You may need to click a folder (📁) to display its contents before you see the program you want to add to the taskbar.

4 Click **Pin to Taskbar**.

■ The program appears on the taskbar.

5 To close the Start menu, click a blank area on your screen.

REORDER PROGRAMS ON TASKBAR

1 To reorder the programs on the taskbar, position the mouse ⍉ over a program you want to move.

2 Drag the program to a new location on the taskbar.

ADJUST THE VOLUME

You can adjust the volume of sound on your computer.

Windows allows you to easily adjust the volume of your speakers. You can also adjust the volume of individual devices and programs on your computer without affecting the volume of other devices and programs.

ADJUST THE SPEAKER VOLUME

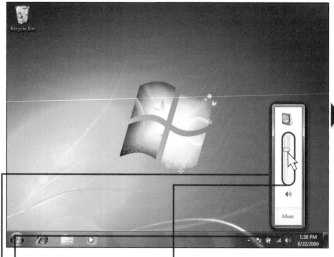

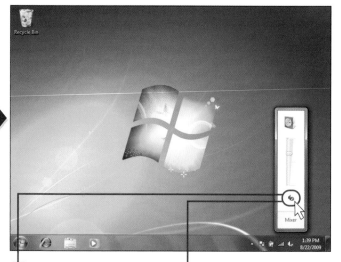

1 Click 🔊 to display the Volume control.

■ The Volume control appears.

2 To adjust the speaker volume, drag the slider (⬜) up or down to increase or decrease the volume.

Note: As you drag the slider (⬜), the number beside the slider indicates the speaker volume strength as a percentage from 0 to 100 percent.

3 To turn off the sound coming from your speakers, click 🔊 (🔊 changes to 🔇).

Note: When you turn off the sound, the speaker icon 🔊 on the taskbar changes to 🔇 .

■ To once again turn on the sound, click 🔇 (🔇 changes to 🔊).

4 When you finish adjusting the speaker volume, click a blank area on your desktop to hide the Volume control.

Tip

What devices and programs can appear in the Volume Mixer dialog box?

The devices and programs that appear in the Volume Mixer dialog box depend on the devices that are connected to your computer and the programs you have open that produce sound. Here are some devices and programs you can see in the dialog box.

Speakers—Adjusts the volume of your speakers.

System Sounds—Adjusts the volume of sounds that play when certain events, such as the arrival of new e-mail messages, occur on your computer.

Windows Media Player—Adjusts the sounds playing in Windows Media Player.

Tip

Is there another way that I can adjust the speaker volume?

Yes. Many speakers have a volume control that you can use to adjust the volume. Your speakers may also have a power button that you can use to turn the sound on or off. If you are using a laptop computer, the computer will usually have keys that you can press to adjust the volume of the computer's speakers.

ADJUST THE VOLUME OF INDIVIDUAL DEVICES

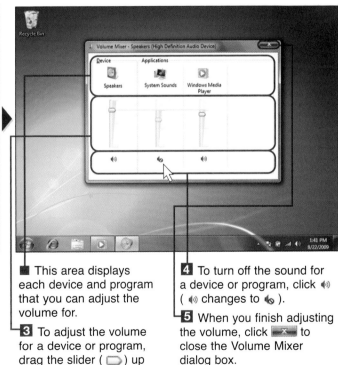

1 Click 🔊 to display the Volume control.

■ The Volume control appears.

2 Click **Mixer** to adjust the volume of individual devices and programs on your computer.

■ The Volume Mixer dialog box appears.

■ This area displays each device and program that you can adjust the volume for.

3 To adjust the volume for a device or program, drag the slider (▭) up or down to increase or decrease the volume.

4 To turn off the sound for a device or program, click 🔊 (🔊 changes to 🔇).

5 When you finish adjusting the volume, click ☒ to close the Volume Mixer dialog box.

CHANGE THE COMPUTER SOUNDS

You can change the sounds that your computer plays when certain events occur on your computer. For example, you can hear a short tune when you log on to Windows.

You can change the sounds that your computer plays for many events at once by selecting a sound scheme. A sound scheme consists of a set of related sounds.

CHANGE THE COMPUTER SOUNDS

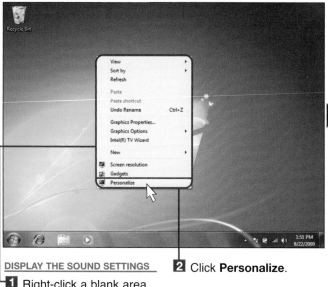

DISPLAY THE SOUND SETTINGS

1 Right-click a blank area on your desktop. A menu appears.

2 Click **Personalize**.

■ The Personalization window appears.

3 Click **Sounds** to change your computer's sounds.

■ The Sound dialog box appears.

Tip

What events can Windows play sounds for?

Windows can play sounds for more than 45 events on your computer. Here are some examples.

Close Program—A sound will play each time you close a program.

Device Connect—A sound will play each time you connect a device to your computer.

Exit Windows—A sound will play each time you exit Windows.

New Mail Notification—A sound will play each time you receive a new e-mail message.

Print Complete—A sound will play when the printing of a file is complete.

Windows Logon—A sound will play each time you log on to Windows.

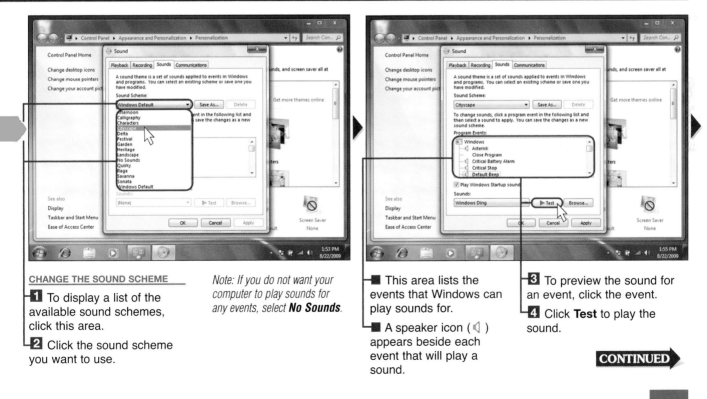

CHANGE THE SOUND SCHEME

1 To display a list of the available sound schemes, click this area.

2 Click the sound scheme you want to use.

*Note: If you do not want your computer to play sounds for any events, select **No Sounds**.*

■ This area lists the events that Windows can play sounds for.

■ A speaker icon (◁) appears beside each event that will play a sound.

3 To preview the sound for an event, click the event.

4 Click **Test** to play the sound.

CONTINUED ▶

CHANGE THE COMPUTER SOUNDS

When changing the sounds that your computer plays, you can select sounds that you want to play when certain events occur.

For example, you may want to play a sound clip or music from your favorite cartoon when you close a program or hear a sigh of relief when you exit Windows.

You can use the sounds included with Windows or obtain sounds on the Internet. The sounds you use must be in the Wave format. Wave files have the .wav extension, such as chimes.wav.

CHANGE THE COMPUTER SOUNDS (CONTINUED)

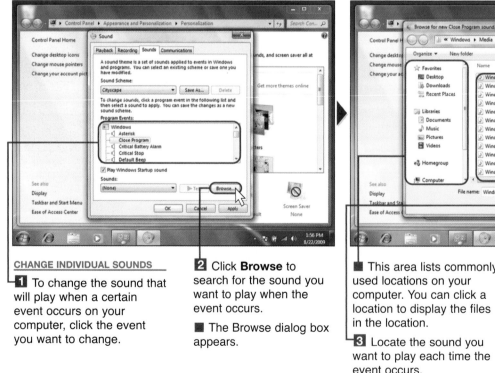

CHANGE INDIVIDUAL SOUNDS

1 To change the sound that will play when a certain event occurs on your computer, click the event you want to change.

2 Click **Browse** to search for the sound you want to play when the event occurs.

■ The Browse dialog box appears.

■ This area lists commonly used locations on your computer. You can click a location to display the files in the location.

3 Locate the sound you want to play each time the event occurs.

4 Click the sound.

5 Click **Open** to confirm your selection.

168

Tip

How can I stop a sound from playing when a certain event occurs on my computer?

In the Sound dialog box, click the event you no longer want to play a sound. Click ▼ below Sounds: and then select **(None)** from the top of the list.

Tip

Can I save the changes I make to my computer's sounds?

Yes. After you select the sounds you want to play for certain events on your computer, you can save your changes as a new sound scheme. In the Sound dialog box, click **Save As**. Type a name for your new sound scheme and then click **OK**. The sound scheme will appear in the list of available sound schemes.

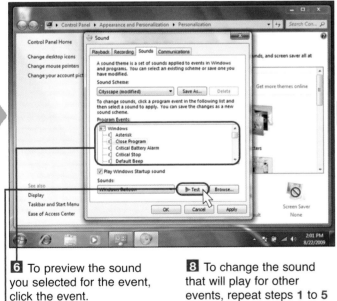

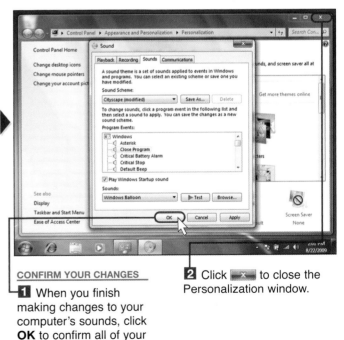

6 To preview the sound you selected for the event, click the event.

7 Click **Test** to test the sound.

8 To change the sound that will play for other events, repeat steps **1** to **5** for each event.

CONFIRM YOUR CHANGES

1 When you finish making changes to your computer's sounds, click **OK** to confirm all of your changes.

2 Click ✕ to close the Personalization window.

VIEW AND CHANGE THE DATE AND TIME

You can view and change your computer's date and time settings. Windows uses the date and time to record when you create and update your files.

Your computer has a built-in clock that keeps track of the date and time even when you turn off your computer.

To help ensure that your computer's clock is accurate, Windows automatically synchronizes your computer's clock with a time server on the Internet about once a week. Your computer must be connected to the Internet for the synchronization to occur.

VIEW THE DATE AND TIME

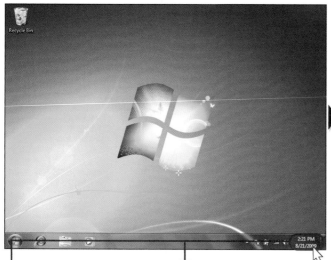

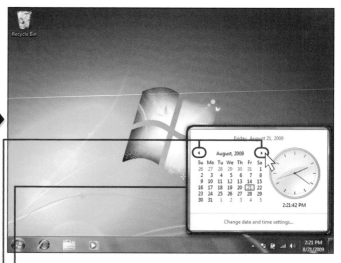

■ This area displays the time and date.

1 To view a calendar, click the time or date.

■ A calendar appears, displaying the days in the current month. The current day appears in blue and displays a border.

2 To browse through the months in the calendar, click ◀ or ▶ to display the previous or next month.

3 When you finish viewing the calendar, click a blank area on your screen to close the calendar.

How do I change the date and time?

To change the date and time, click **Change date and time** in the Date and Time dialog box. If you do not have an administrator account, you will need to type an administrator password and then click **Yes** to be able to continue. In the dialog box that appears, click the correct day and then double-click the part of the time you want to change and type the correct time. Click **OK** to save your changes.

Tip **How do I change the time zone?**

To change the time zone, click **Change time zone** in the Date and Time dialog box. In the dialog box that appears, select a time zone from the list of available time zones and then click **OK** to save your change. You may want to change the time zone when traveling or after you move to a new city.

VIEW THE DATE AND TIME SETTINGS

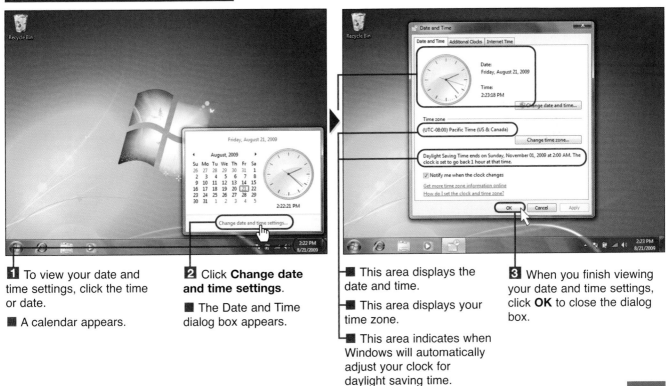

1 To view your date and time settings, click the time or date.

■ A calendar appears.

2 Click **Change date and time settings**.

■ The Date and Time dialog box appears.

■ This area displays the date and time.

■ This area displays your time zone.

■ This area indicates when Windows will automatically adjust your clock for daylight saving time.

3 When you finish viewing your date and time settings, click **OK** to close the dialog box.

ADD A BLUETOOTH DEVICE

You can add a Bluetooth device to your computer so you can use the device with your computer.

Bluetooth wireless technology allows computers and devices, such as a mouse, keyboard, headset, mobile phone or printer, to communicate without cables. Bluetooth devices use radio signals to transmit information.

PREPARE A BLUETOOTH DEVICE

■ Before adding a Bluetooth device to your computer, make sure the device is ready to be added.

1 Insert batteries into the Bluetooth device.

2 Turn the Bluetooth device on.

3 If you are adding a Bluetooth mouse or keyboard to a desktop computer, make sure a mouse or keyboard is currently connected to the computer. You will need to use this mouse or keyboard to add the Bluetooth mouse or keyboard to the computer.

4 Make sure the Bluetooth device is discoverable, which means that your computer can detect the device.

■ If you are adding a Bluetooth mouse or keyboard, you will usually find a button at the bottom of the device that you can press to make the device discoverable.

Note: To determine how to make your Bluetooth device discoverable, refer to the documentation that came with your device or visit the manufacturer's website.

Can my computer use Bluetooth devices?

Some computers come with built-in capability to use Bluetooth devices, especially laptop computers. If your computer does not come with the capability to use Bluetooth devices, you can add the capability by plugging a Bluetooth adapter into a USB port on your computer. After you add Bluetooth capability to your computer, any Bluetooth device can communicate with your computer.

Note: If you have a laptop computer with built-in Bluetooth capability, make sure the Bluetooth radio transmitter is turned on. Many laptop computers have an external switch for turning the transmitter on and off.

What else do I need to do to prepare a Bluetooth device?

✓ Make sure the Bluetooth device is not low on battery power, in sleep or standby mode and has Bluetooth power turned on.

✓ Make sure the Bluetooth device is within range of your computer, typically within 6 to 9 feet.

✓ Make sure there are no other devices that could interfere with the Bluetooth device, such as a microwave oven, cordless phone or other wireless device.

ADD A BLUETOOTH DEVICE

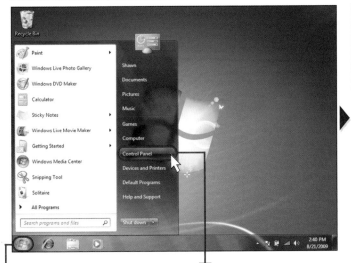

■ In this example, we are adding a Bluetooth keyboard to a computer.

1 Click 🟠 to display the Start menu.

2 Click **Control Panel** to access your computer's settings.

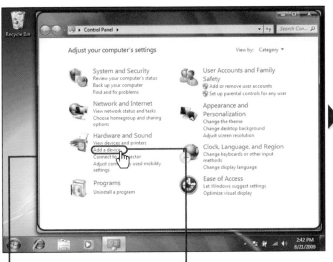

■ The Control Panel window appears.

3 Click **Add a device** to add a Bluetooth device to your computer.

CONTINUED

Share Your Computer

CREATE A USER ACCOUNT

If you share your computer with other people, you can create a personalized user account for each person.

Even if you do not share your computer with other people, Microsoft recommends that you create a standard user account and use that account instead of the administrator account that was automatically set up when Windows was installed.

CREATE A USER ACCOUNT

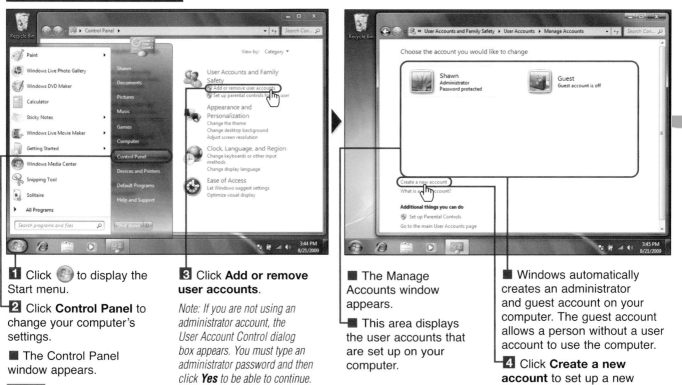

1 Click 🔵 to display the Start menu.

2 Click **Control Panel** to change your computer's settings.

■ The Control Panel window appears.

3 Click **Add or remove user accounts**.

*Note: If you are not using an administrator account, the User Account Control dialog box appears. You must type an administrator password and then click **Yes** to be able to continue.*

■ The Manage Accounts window appears.

■ This area displays the user accounts that are set up on your computer.

■ Windows automatically creates an administrator and guest account on your computer. The guest account allows a person without a user account to use the computer.

4 Click **Create a new account** to set up a new account on your computer.

Tip

What types of user accounts can I create?

Standard user—You can perform almost any task on the computer. However, you cannot perform tasks that affect other users or the security of the computer without first entering an administrator password. Microsoft recommends that you create a standard account for each user.

Administrator—You can perform any task on the computer. Microsoft does not recommend this type of account for daily use.

Tip

Will Windows keep my personal files separate from the files of other users?

Yes. Windows will keep your personal files separate from the personal files created by other users. For example, your Documents, Pictures and Music libraries display the files you have created. Internet Explorer also keeps your lists of recently visited webpages and favorite webpages separate from the lists of other users.

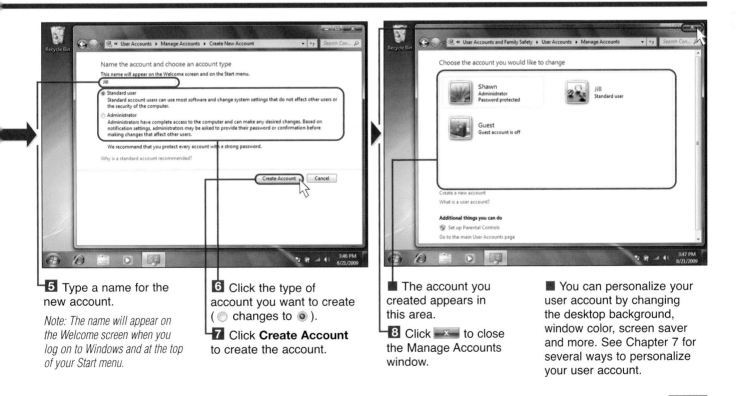

5 Type a name for the new account.

Note: The name will appear on the Welcome screen when you log on to Windows and at the top of your Start menu.

6 Click the type of account you want to create (○ changes to ◉).

7 Click **Create Account** to create the account.

■ The account you created appears in this area.

8 Click [X] to close the Manage Accounts window.

■ You can personalize your user account by changing the desktop background, window color, screen saver and more. See Chapter 7 for several ways to personalize your user account.

DELETE A USER ACCOUNT

If a person no longer uses your computer, you can delete the person's user account from your computer.

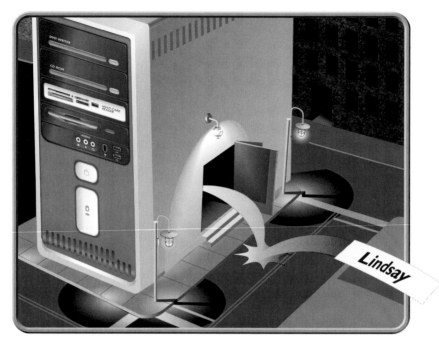

DELETE A USER ACCOUNT

1 Click ● to display the Start menu.

2 Click **Control Panel** to change your computer's settings.

■ The Control Panel window appears.

3 Click **Add or remove user accounts**.

Note: If you are not using an administrator account, the User Account Control dialog box appears. You must type an administrator password and then click Yes to be able to continue.

■ The Manage Accounts window appears.

■ This area displays the user accounts that are set up on your computer.

4 Click the user account you want to delete.

Note: You cannot delete the Guest account, which allows a person without a user account to use your computer.

Tip

When I delete a user account, which personal files can Windows save?

When you delete a user account, Windows can save the user's personal files that are displayed on the desktop and the files in the My Documents, My Music, My Pictures and My Videos folders. Windows will also save the user's list of favorite webpages. The files will be saved on your desktop in a new folder that has the same name as the deleted account. Windows will not save the user's e-mail messages or computer settings.

Tip

Can I delete an administrator account?

Yes. You can delete administrator accounts. However, Windows will not allow you to delete the last administrator account on your computer. This ensures that one administrator account always exists on the computer.

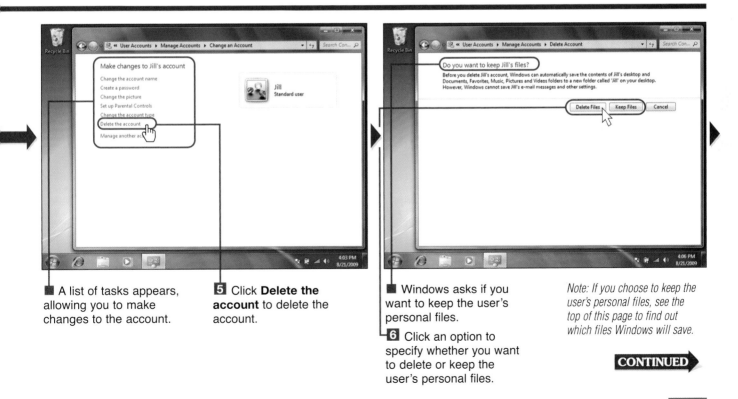

■ A list of tasks appears, allowing you to make changes to the account.

5 Click **Delete the account** to delete the account.

■ Windows asks if you want to keep the user's personal files.

6 Click an option to specify whether you want to delete or keep the user's personal files.

Note: If you choose to keep the user's personal files, see the top of this page to find out which files Windows will save.

CONTINUED

DELETE A USER ACCOUNT

When you delete a user account, Windows will permanently remove the account from your computer.

DELETE A USER ACCOUNT (CONTINUED)

■ Windows asks you to confirm that you want to delete the account.

7 Click **Delete Account** to permanently delete the account.

■ Windows deletes the account from your computer.

8 Click ✕ to close the Manage Accounts window.

SWITCH USERS

If another person wants to use your computer, you can allow the person to switch to their user account. Windows will keep your files and programs open while the other person logs on to Windows and uses the computer.

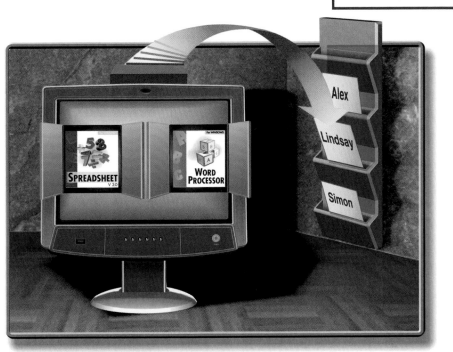

When you switch between users, you can quickly return to your files and programs after the other person finishes using the computer.

SWITCH USERS

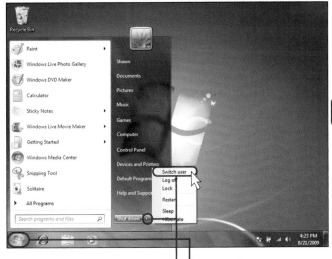

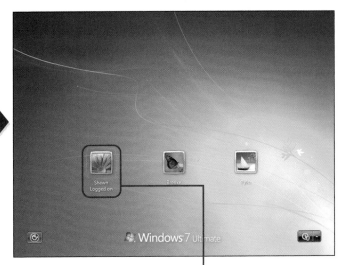

■ Before switching users, you should save any files you have open.

Note: If another person turns off the computer, any unsaved changes you have made to your files will be lost.

1 Click 📶 to display the Start menu.

2 Click ▶ to display a list of options.

3 Click **Switch user**.

■ The Welcome screen appears, allowing another person to log on to Windows to use the computer. To log on to Windows, see page 185.

■ Windows keeps your user account "logged on," which means that your files and programs remain open on the computer.

LOG OFF WINDOWS

When you finish using your computer, you can log off Windows to allow another person to log on to Windows to use the computer.

When you log off Windows, your user account is closed but your computer remains on.

LOG OFF WINDOWS

■ Before logging off Windows, you should close your open files and programs.

1 Click 🔵 to display the Start menu.

2 Click ▶ to display a list of options.

3 Click **Log off** to log off Windows.

■ The Welcome screen appears, allowing another person to log on to Windows to use the computer. To log on to Windows, see page 185.

■ If another person turns off the computer, the person does not need to worry about losing any of your information since your user account is closed.

LOG ON TO WINDOWS

If you have set up user accounts on your computer, you will need to log on to Windows to use the computer.

If you have only one user account set up on your computer and have assigned a password to that account, you will also need to log on to Windows to use the computer. To assign a password to a user account, see page 186.

LOG ON TO WINDOWS

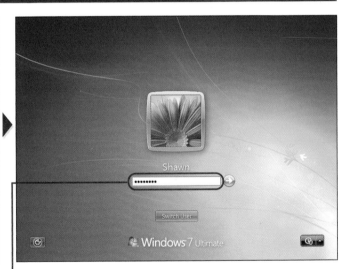

■ When you turn on your computer, switch user accounts or log off Windows, the Welcome screen appears.

■ This area displays the user accounts set up on your computer.

1 Click the name of your user account.

■ If you assigned a password to your user account, you need to enter your password to log on to Windows.

2 Type your password and then press the **Enter** key.

*Note: A message appears if you enter the wrong password. Click **OK** to try entering the password again. This time, Windows will display the password hint you entered when you created the password.*

■ Windows starts, displaying your personal files and computer settings.

CREATE A PASSWORD

You can add a password to your user account to prevent other people from accessing the account. You will need to enter the password each time you want to log on to Windows.

If your password contains capital letters, you will need to type the letters in the same way each time you enter your password.

When you create a password, you can enter a password hint that can help you remember the password. The hint will be available to everyone who uses the computer. To display a password hint, see page 185.

CREATE A PASSWORD

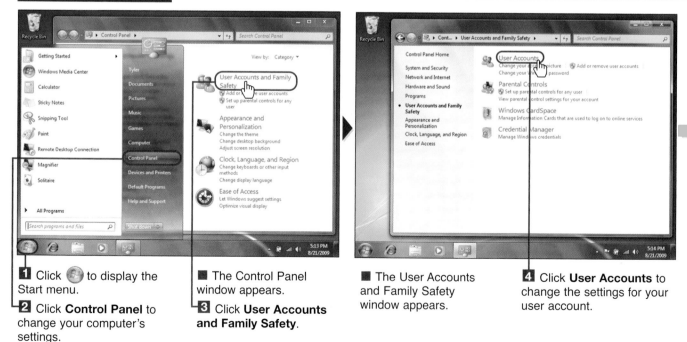

1 Click  to display the Start menu.

2 Click **Control Panel** to change your computer's settings.

■ The Control Panel window appears.

3 Click **User Accounts and Family Safety**.

■ The User Accounts and Family Safety window appears.

4 Click **User Accounts** to change the settings for your user account.

Tip

How do I create a good password?

A good password:

✓ Contains at least eight characters.

✓ Contains uppercase letters (A,B,C), lowercase letters (a,b,c), numbers (0,1,2,3) as well as symbols found on the keyboard (!,@,#,$,%) or spaces.

✓ Does not contain your real name, company name or user name.

✓ Does not contain a complete word.

✓ Is easy to remember, such as:
Msb=8/Apr 94 ➜ "My son's birthday is
                        April 8, 1994"
iL2e CwDp! ➜ "I like to eat chips with dip!"

Tip

How do I change my password?

To change your password, perform steps **1** to **4** below and then click **Change your password**. Type the current password and the new password you want to use. Then type the new password again to confirm the password. If you want to provide a password hint, type the hint and then click **Change password** to change the password.

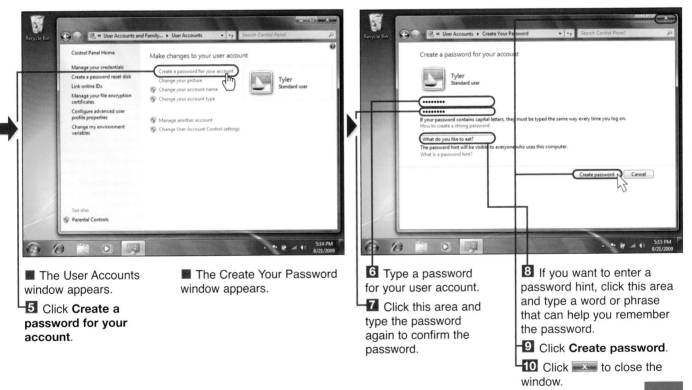

■ The User Accounts window appears.

5 Click **Create a password for your account**.

■ The Create Your Password window appears.

6 Type a password for your user account.

7 Click this area and type the password again to confirm the password.

8 If you want to enter a password hint, click this area and type a word or phrase that can help you remember the password.

9 Click **Create password**.

10 Click ⨯ to close the window.

SHARE FILES WITH OTHER USERS

You can share files with other users set up on your computer by adding files to one of the Public folders. Every user on your computer can access the files stored in the Public folders.

You will find a Public folder in each of your libraries. Windows offers a Public Documents, Public Music, Public Pictures and Public Videos folder.

SHARE FILES WITH OTHER USERS

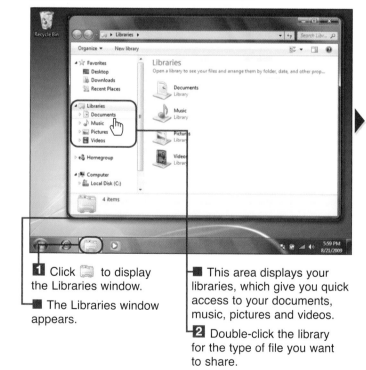

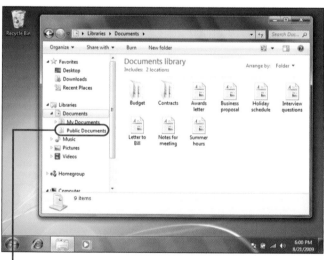

1 Click 📁 to display the Libraries window.

■ The Libraries window appears.

■ This area displays your libraries, which give you quick access to your documents, music, pictures and videos.

2 Double-click the library for the type of file you want to share.

■ The Public folder for the library appears. The Public folder stores the files shared by every user on your computer.

Note: Windows offers a Public Documents, Public Music, Public Pictures and Public Videos folder.

Tip

How can I see the files shared by other users on my computer?

In each library, you will see the files shared by other users on your computer as well as your own personal files. Each library displays the contents of two folders. For example, the Documents library displays the contents of the My Documents folder, which contains your personal files, and the Public Documents folder, which contains the files shared by every user on your computer.

Tip

How do I no longer share a file on my computer?

If you no longer want to share a file with other users on your computer, you need to move the file out of the Public folder. To do so, repeat steps **1** to **5** below, except drag the file to the My Documents, My Music, My Pictures or My Videos folder. Only you can see the files in these folders.

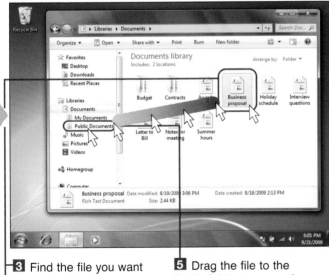

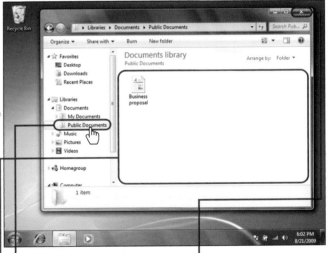

3 Find the file you want to share with other users on your computer.

4 Position the mouse over the file.

5 Drag the file to the Public folder to move the file to the folder.

6 To share additional files, repeat steps **2** to **5** for each file you want to share.

7 To view the contents of a Public folder, click the folder.

■ This area displays the contents of the Public folder. Every user on your computer can open, edit and delete the files stored in a Public folder.

8 When you finish sharing files, click to close the window.

SET UP PARENTAL CONTROLS

You can set up parental controls to help control how your children use your computer.

You can set up time limits to control when your children can use the computer. You can also control which games your children can play and the programs they can use.

Before setting up parental controls, make sure your administrator accounts are password protected to prevent your children from bypassing or turning off parental controls. To create a password, see page 186.

SET UP PARENTAL CONTROLS

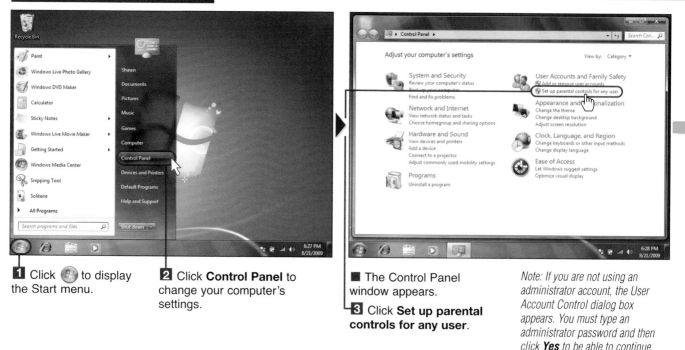

1 Click to display the Start menu.

2 Click **Control Panel** to change your computer's settings.

■ The Control Panel window appears.

3 Click **Set up parental controls for any user**.

*Note: If you are not using an administrator account, the User Account Control dialog box appears. You must type an administrator password and then click **Yes** to be able to continue.*

Tip **Why is web filtering and activity reporting not available on my computer?**

Web filtering and activity reporting are not included in Windows 7. Web filtering allows you to limit the websites your children can visit. Activity reporting collects information about your children's computer activities, such as the websites visited and the total time spent on the computer. For information on how to add these features, you can click **How do I install additional controls?** at the bottom of the Parental Controls window.

Tip **How do I turn off parental controls?**

To turn off parental controls for a child, perform steps **1** to **3** below and then click the child's user account in the window that appears. Below Parental Controls, click **Off** and then click **OK** to save your changes. You now no longer control how your child uses the computer.

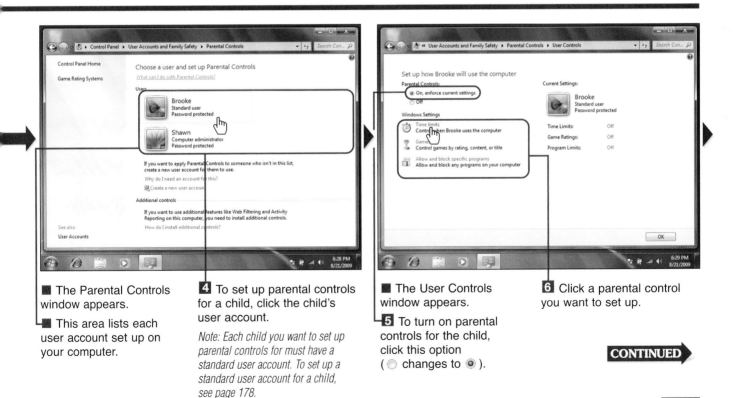

■ The Parental Controls window appears.

■ This area lists each user account set up on your computer.

4 To set up parental controls for a child, click the child's user account.

Note: Each child you want to set up parental controls for must have a standard user account. To set up a standard user account for a child, see page 178.

■ The User Controls window appears.

5 To turn on parental controls for the child, click this option (○ changes to ◉).

6 Click a parental control you want to set up.

CONTINUED

SET UP PARENTAL CONTROLS

You can set up time limits to control when your children can use the computer.

You can also specify which programs your children can use. For example, you can prevent your children from opening a program that you use to keep track of your finances.

SET UP PARENTAL CONTROLS (CONTINUED)

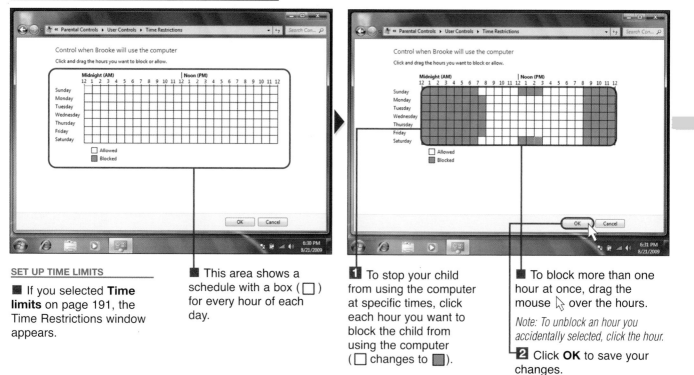

SET UP TIME LIMITS

■ If you selected **Time limits** on page 191, the Time Restrictions window appears.

■ This area shows a schedule with a box (☐) for every hour of each day.

1 To stop your child from using the computer at specific times, click each hour you want to block the child from using the computer (☐ changes to ▨).

■ To block more than one hour at once, drag the mouse ▷ over the hours.

Note: To unblock an hour you accidentally selected, click the hour.

2 Click **OK** to save your changes.

Tip

What else can I do to help protect my children when they use the computer?

Although the Parental Controls feature included with Windows can help manage how your children use the computer, it should not replace parental supervision. Constant adult supervision is the best way to help protect your children. Here are some tips:

✓ Keep the family computer in a high-traffic area in your house, such as the kitchen or family room, so you can monitor all activity.

✓ Maintain an ongoing conversation with your children about their computer activities.

✓ Tell your children not to provide their photo or personal information, such as their name, address, phone number or school name, to anyone they meet on the Internet.

✓ Tell your children not to meet with anyone they have met on the Internet.

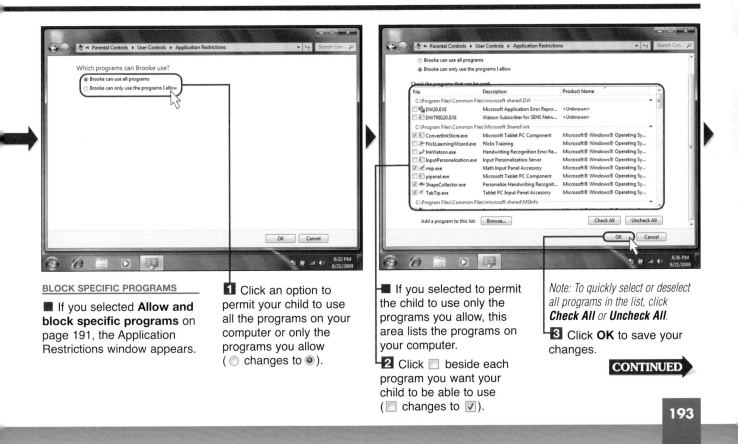

BLOCK SPECIFIC PROGRAMS

■ If you selected **Allow and block specific programs** on page 191, the Application Restrictions window appears.

1 Click an option to permit your child to use all the programs on your computer or only the programs you allow (○ changes to ◉).

■ If you selected to permit the child to use only the programs you allow, this area lists the programs on your computer.

2 Click ☐ beside each program you want your child to be able to use (☐ changes to ☑).

Note: To quickly select or deselect all programs in the list, click ***Check All*** *or* ***Uncheck All***.

3 Click **OK** to save your changes.

CONTINUED

SET UP PARENTAL CONTROLS

You can control which games your children can play on your computer. For example, you can block your children from playing a game that is not age appropriate.

Most games sold in stores are rated to help you determine which games are appropriate for your children. You can look on a game's box for the game's rating.

SET UP PARENTAL CONTROLS (CONTINUED)

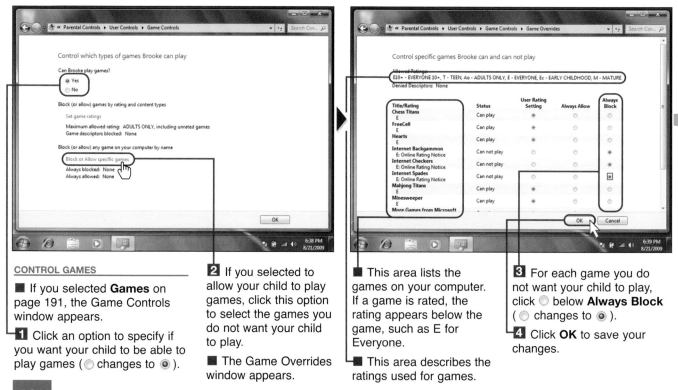

CONTROL GAMES

■ If you selected **Games** on page 191, the Game Controls window appears.

1 Click an option to specify if you want your child to be able to play games (◯ changes to ◉).

2 If you selected to allow your child to play games, click this option to select the games you do not want your child to play.

■ The Game Overrides window appears.

■ This area lists the games on your computer. If a game is rated, the rating appears below the game, such as E for Everyone.

■ This area describes the ratings used for games.

3 For each game you do not want your child to play, click ◯ below **Always Block** (◯ changes to ◉).

4 Click **OK** to save your changes.

194

Tip

Can I use game ratings to control which games my child can play?

Yes. In the Game Controls window, click **Yes** to allow your child to play games and then click **Set game ratings**. In the window that appears, click a game rating that is appropriate for your child. At the top of the window, click an option to allow or block games with no rating. Click **OK** to save your changes. Your child can now play only the games with the rating you selected.

 Tip

How can I help keep my children safer online?

With the Family Safety program, you can block certain websites, limit searches, monitor the websites your children visit and choose who your children can communicate with. You can obtain the Family Safety program for free at the Windows Live Essentials website (http://download.live.com). For more information on this website, see page 50.

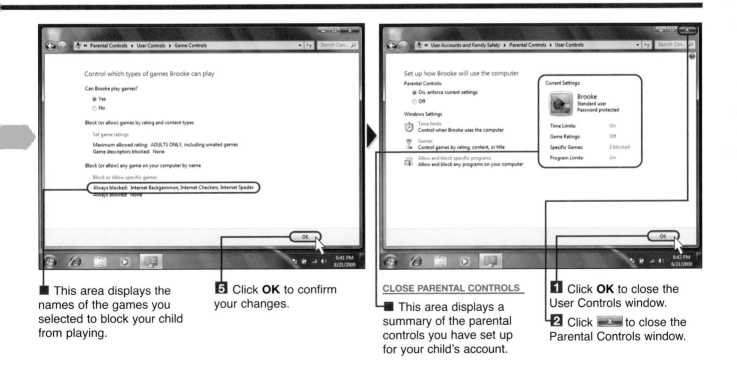

■ This area displays the names of the games you selected to block your child from playing.

5 Click **OK** to confirm your changes.

CLOSE PARENTAL CONTROLS

■ This area displays a summary of the parental controls you have set up for your child's account.

1 Click **OK** to close the User Controls window.

2 Click ▨ to close the Parental Controls window.

Browse the Web

START INTERNET EXPLORER

You can start Internet Explorer to browse through the information on the web.

You need a connection to the Internet to browse through the information on the web.

START INTERNET EXPLORER

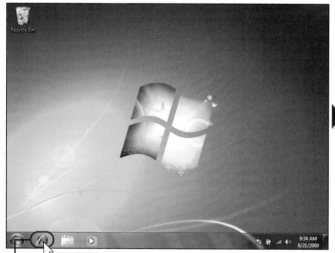

1 Click 🖉 to start Internet Explorer.

Note: The first time you start Internet Explorer, a welcome dialog box appears, allowing you to choose your settings. Follow the instructions in the dialog box to choose your settings.

■ The Windows Internet Explorer window appears, displaying your home page.

Note: Your home page is the webpage that appears each time you start Internet Explorer. To change your home page, see page 208.

2 When you finish browsing the web, click ✕ to close Internet Explorer.

You can display any webpage on the Internet that you have heard or read about.

Every webpage has a unique address. You need to know the address of a webpage you want to view.

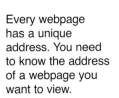

Internet Explorer blocks pop-up windows, which are small windows that often display advertisements and usually appear as soon as you visit a website.

Internet Explorer also blocks content that might not be safe. For example, a website may try to collect information about you, download harmful files or install software without your consent.

DISPLAY A WEBPAGE

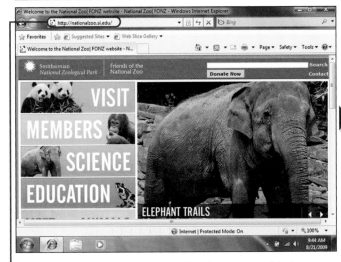

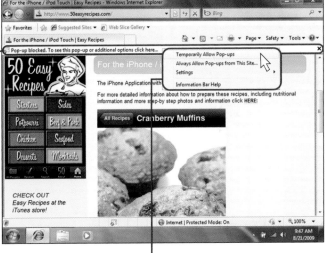

1 Click this area to highlight the current webpage address.

2 Type the address of the webpage you want to display and then press the **Enter** key.

Note: As you type, a list of matching webpages that you have recently viewed appears. If you want to display a webpage on the list, click the webpage.

■ The webpage appears on your screen.

VIEW BLOCKED CONTENT

■ The Information bar appears when Internet Explorer blocks a pop-up window or blocks content that might not be safe.

1 If you want to view, download or install the blocked content, click the Information bar. A menu appears.

2 Click the option that allows you to unblock the content.

There are many ways that you can work with webpages in Internet Explorer. For example, when viewing a webpage, you can select a link to display related information.

A link connects text or an image on one webpage to another webpage. When you select the text or image, the linked webpage appears.

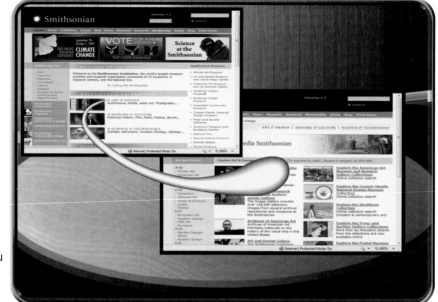

When working with webpages, you can also move back and forward through webpages you have viewed and stop the transfer of a webpage to your computer. You can also refresh a webpage to transfer a fresh copy of the webpage to your computer.

SELECT A LINK

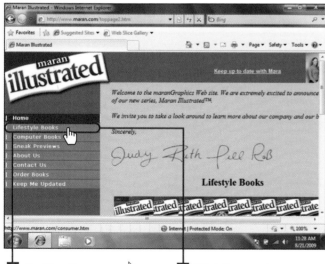

1 Position the mouse over a word or image of interest. The mouse changes to a hand when it is over a link.

2 Click the word or image to display the linked webpage.

■ The linked webpage will appear.

Note: In some cases, clicking a link will display a menu instead of a webpage.

MOVE THROUGH WEBPAGES

MOVE BACK

1 Click ◀ to return to the last webpage you viewed.

Note: The ◀ button is only available if you have viewed more than one webpage since you last started Internet Explorer.

MOVE FORWARD

1 Click ▶ to move forward through the webpages you have viewed.

Note: The ▶ button is only available after you use the ◀ button to return to a webpage.

Tip

Can I make a webpage larger?

Yes. If you have trouble reading small text on a webpage, you can enlarge a webpage. At the bottom-right corner of the Internet Explorer window, click ▼ beside 🔍 100%. Click the zoom percentage you want to use on the menu that appears.

 Tip

How can I make a webpage look better?

Webpages designed for an earlier version of Internet Explorer may not appear correctly. If Internet Explorer recognizes that a webpage was designed for an earlier version of Internet Explorer, 📄 appears at the top of the Internet Explorer window beside the Refresh button (🔄). You can click 📄 to improve how the webpage looks. To turn the feature off, click 📄 again.

STOP TRANSFER OF A WEBPAGE

■ If a webpage is taking a long time to appear on your screen or contains information that does not interest you, you can stop the transfer of the webpage.

1 Click ✕ to stop the transfer of the webpage.

REFRESH A WEBPAGE

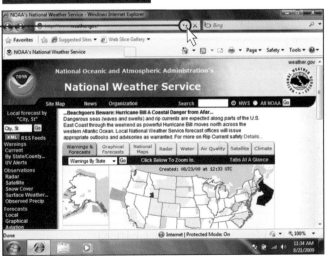

■ You can refresh a webpage to transfer a fresh copy of the webpage to your computer.

1 Click 🔄 to refresh the webpage displayed on your screen.

■ Refreshing a webpage is useful for updating webpages that contain regularly changing information, such as news or images from a live camera.

PRINT A WEBPAGE

You can produce a paper copy of a webpage displayed on your screen. Before printing a webpage, you can preview how the webpage will look when printed.

PREVIEW A WEBPAGE BEFORE PRINTING

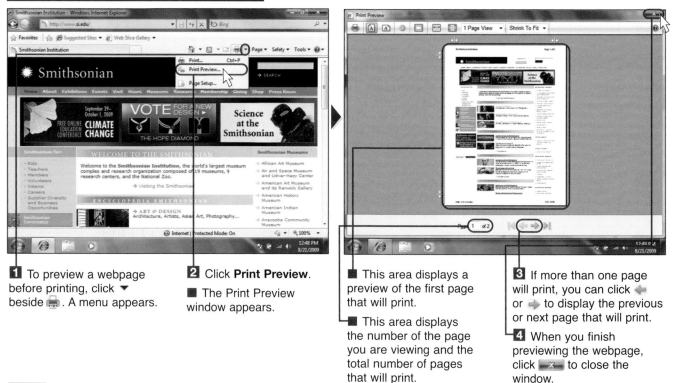

1 To preview a webpage before printing, click ▼ beside 🖨. A menu appears.

2 Click **Print Preview**.

■ The Print Preview window appears.

■ This area displays a preview of the first page that will print.

■ This area displays the number of the page you are viewing and the total number of pages that will print.

3 If more than one page will print, you can click ⬅ or ➡ to display the previous or next page that will print.

4 When you finish previewing the webpage, click ✖ to close the window.

Tip

Why does the text on a webpage appear so small when it prints?

When you print a webpage, Internet Explorer shrinks the content of the webpage to fit across a piece of paper. This prevents the right side of a webpage from being cut off, but may make the text smaller and more difficult to read. To print the content of a webpage at a larger size, you can click 🅐 in the Print Preview window to change to the landscape orientation. This will print the content of a webpage across the longer side of your paper.

Note: If you want to return to the portrait orientation, click 🅐 in the Print Preview window.

Tip

Can I print only specific pages of a webpage?

Yes. After previewing how a webpage will print, you may want to print only specific pages. In the Print Preview window, click 🖶. The Print dialog box appears, displaying options you can select for printing the webpage. Double-click the number beside **Pages** and then type the pages you want to print, such as 1 or 2-4. Then click **Print** to print the pages.

PRINT A WEBPAGE

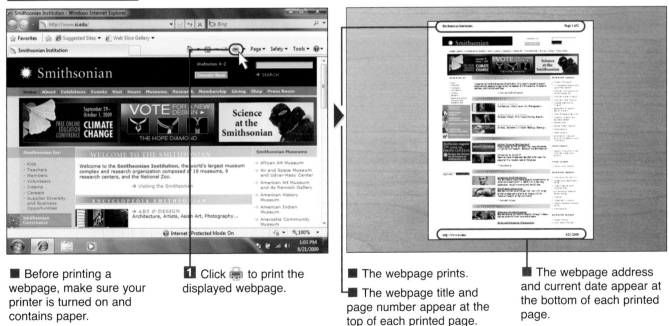

■ Before printing a webpage, make sure your printer is turned on and contains paper.

1 Click 🖶 to print the displayed webpage.

■ The webpage prints.

■ The webpage title and page number appear at the top of each printed page.

■ The webpage address and current date appear at the bottom of each printed page.

SEARCH THE WEB

You can search for webpages that discuss topics of interest to you.

Websites that allow you to search for information on the web are known as search providers. Internet Explorer uses Bing to search for information on the web. You can add other search providers, such as Google and Yahoo!, to your list of available search providers.

SEARCH THE WEB

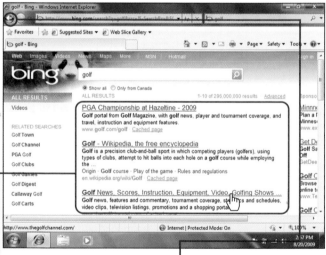

1 Click this area and then type the word or phrase you want to search for. Press the `Enter` key to start the search.

■ As you type, a list of search suggestions appears as well as a list of matching webpages that you have recently viewed. If you want to use a search suggestion to perform the search or display a webpage on the list, click the item.

■ A list of matching webpages appears.

2 To display a webpage of interest, click the title of the webpage.

■ The webpage you selected will appear.

■ You can click ⊙ to return to the list of webpages and select another page.

Tip

How do I change which search provider is used?

Before performing a search, click ▾ beside the search box and then click the search provider you want to use from the top of the menu that appears. Internet Explorer will use the search provider you select to perform searches until you close Internet Explorer.

Tip

How do I change the default search provider?

You can change which search provider you want to use for all of your searches. Click ▾ beside the search box and then click **Manage Search Providers** on the menu that appears. In the Manage Add-ons dialog box that appears, click the search provider you want to use for all of your searches and then click **Set as default**. Click **Close** to close the dialog box.

ADD A SEARCH PROVIDER

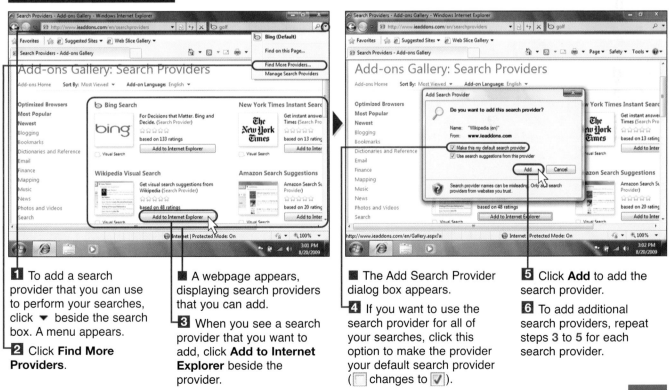

1 To add a search provider that you can use to perform your searches, click ▾ beside the search box. A menu appears.

2 Click **Find More Providers**.

■ A webpage appears, displaying search providers that you can add.

3 When you see a search provider that you want to add, click **Add to Internet Explorer** beside the provider.

■ The Add Search Provider dialog box appears.

4 If you want to use the search provider for all of your searches, click this option to make the provider your default search provider (☐ changes to ☑).

5 Click **Add** to add the search provider.

6 To add additional search providers, repeat steps 3 to 5 for each search provider.

DISPLAY AND CHANGE YOUR HOME PAGE

You can display and change the webpage that appears each time you start Internet Explorer. This webpage is called your home page.

Internet Explorer allows you to have more than one home page. If you set up multiple home pages, also known as home page tabs, each page will appear on its own tab when you start Internet Explorer. For information on tabs, see page 202.

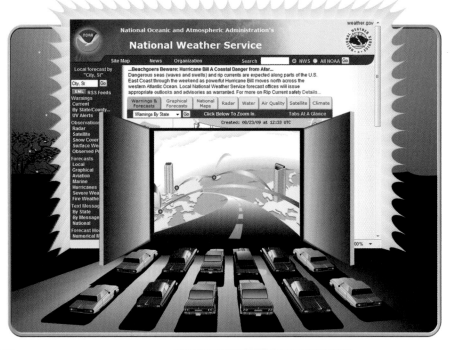

DISPLAY YOUR HOME PAGE

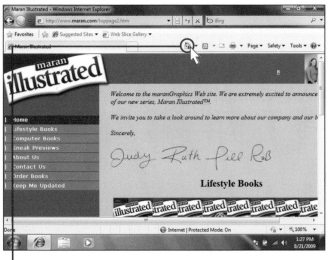

1 Click 🏠 to display your home page.

■ Your home page appears.

CHANGE YOUR HOME PAGE

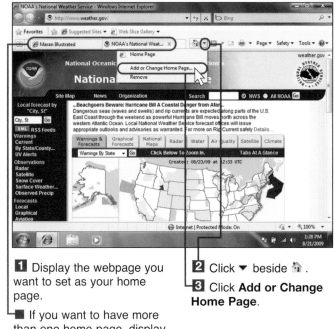

1 Display the webpage you want to set as your home page.

■ If you want to have more than one home page, display each webpage on a separate tab. For information on tabs, see page 202.

2 Click ▼ beside 🏠.

3 Click **Add or Change Home Page**.

Tip

Which webpage should I set as a home page?

You can set any page on the web as a home page. A webpage you choose should be a page you want to frequently visit. You may want to choose a webpage that provides a good starting point for exploring the web, such as www.google.com, or a page that provides information relevant to your personal interests or work.

Tip

How do I remove a home page?

To remove a home page, click ▼ beside 🏠 and then click **Remove** on the menu that appears. Click the home page you want to remove from your list of home pages. In the confirmation dialog box that appears, click **Yes**. The home page you removed will no longer appear when you start Internet Explorer.

Note: If you remove all of your home pages, a blank page will appear when you start Internet Explorer.

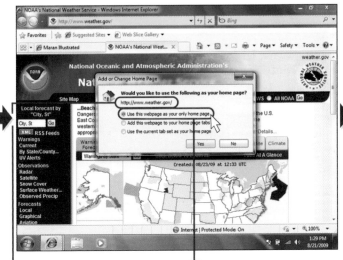

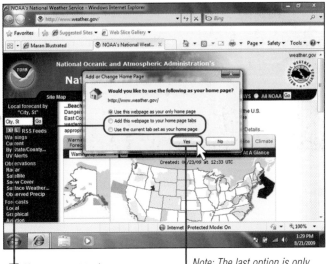

■ The Add or Change Home Page dialog box appears.

■ This area displays the address of the webpage displayed on your screen.

4 Click this option to make the displayed webpage your only home page (◎ changes to ◉).

■ If you want to have more than one home page, click an option to add the displayed webpage to your collection of home pages or make all the webpages you have open your home pages.

Note: The last option is only available if you have more than one tab open.

5 Click **Yes** to confirm your change.

ADD A WEBPAGE TO FAVORITES

You can keep a list of your favorite webpages so you can quickly return to the webpages at any time.

Selecting webpages from your list of favorites saves you from having to remember and constantly retype the same webpage addresses over and over again.

Internet Explorer automatically adds several folders to your list of favorites, including the Microsoft Websites folder, the MSN Websites folder and the Windows Live folder.

ADD A WEBPAGE TO FAVORITES

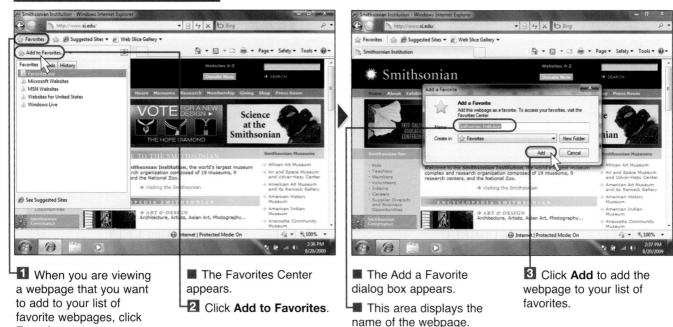

1 When you are viewing a webpage that you want to add to your list of favorite webpages, click **Favorites**.

■ The Favorites Center appears.

2 Click **Add to Favorites**.

■ The Add a Favorite dialog box appears.

■ This area displays the name of the webpage.

3 Click **Add** to add the webpage to your list of favorites.

Tip

How do I move or remove a webpage from my list of favorites?

To move a webpage to a new location in your list of favorites, drag the webpage to a new location in the list.

To remove a webpage from your list of favorites, right-click the webpage in the list and then click **Delete** on the menu that appears. In the confirmation dialog box that appears, click **Yes**.

Tip

Can I create a folder to help organize my list of favorites?

Yes. To create a folder, right-click any folder in your list of favorites and then click **Create New Folder** on the menu that appears. Type a name for the new folder and then press the `Enter` key. To move a favorite webpage into the new folder, drag the webpage in your list of favorites to the folder.

VIEW A FAVORITE WEBPAGE

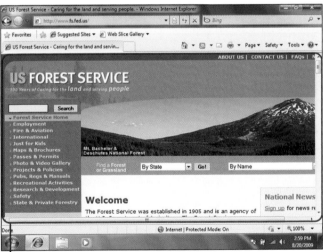

1 Click **Favorites**.

2 Click the **Favorites** tab.

■ A list of your favorite webpages appears.

3 Click the favorite webpage you want to view.

Note: To display the favorite webpages in a folder, click the folder ( ).

■ The favorite webpage you selected appears.

■ You can repeat steps 1 to 3 to view another favorite webpage.

Note: If you want your list of favorite webpages to appear all the time, see the top of page 211.

ADD A WEBPAGE TO THE FAVORITES BAR

You can add your favorite webpages to the Favorites bar so you can instantly return to the webpages. The Favorites bar provides quick access to the webpages you most often visit.

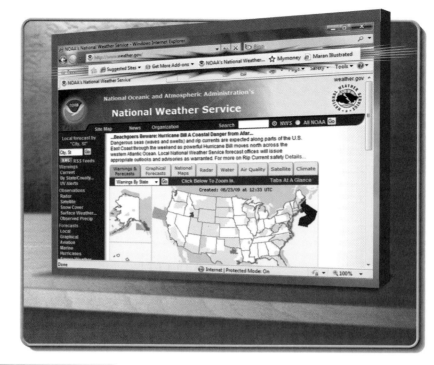

ADD A WEBPAGE TO THE FAVORITES BAR

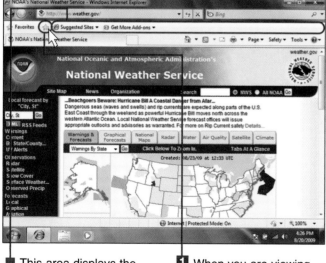

■ This area displays the Favorites bar.

1 When you are viewing a webpage that you want to add to the Favorites bar, click 🌟 .

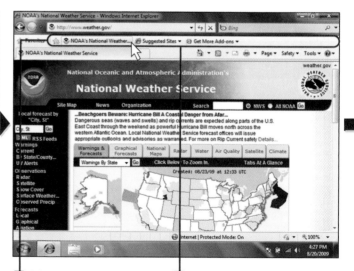

■ A button for the webpage appears on the Favorites bar.

■ To instantly display a webpage you added to the Favorites bar, click the button for the webpage on the Favorites bar.

Tip

What buttons automatically appear on the Favorites bar?

Internet Explorer automatically displays two buttons on the Favorites bar.

The **Suggested Sites** button suggests similar websites that you might be interested in. For more information on the Suggested Sites feature, see page 218.

The **Get More Add-ons** button gives you quick access to extra features that you can add to Internet Explorer.

Note: The Get More Add-ons button initially appears as the Web Slice Gallery button.

Tip

How do I remove a webpage from the Favorites bar?

If you no longer want the button for a webpage to appear on the Favorites bar, right-click the button and then click **Delete** on the menu that appears. In the confirmation dialog box that appears, click **Yes**.

REARRANGE WEBPAGES

1 To rearrange webpages on the Favorites bar, position the mouse ▷ over the button for the webpage that you want to move.

2 Drag the button for the webpage to where you want the button to appear on the Favorites bar.

■ A black line I indicates where the button for the webpage will appear.

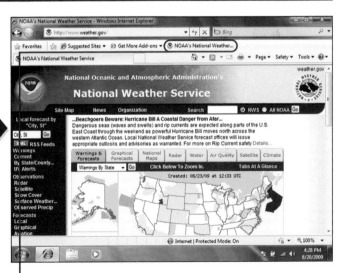

■ The button for the webpage appears in the new location on the Favorites bar.

FIND TEXT ON A WEBPAGE

When viewing a webpage, you can quickly locate a word or phrase of interest on the webpage.

By default, Internet Explorer will find text on a webpage even if the text is part of a larger word. For example, if you search for place, Internet Explorer will also find places, placement and commonplace.

FIND TEXT ON A WEBPAGE

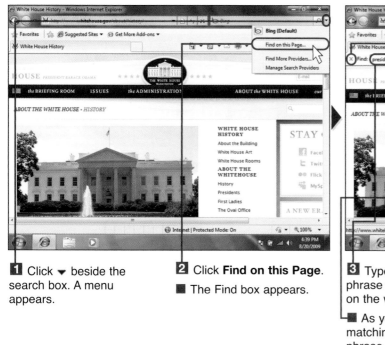

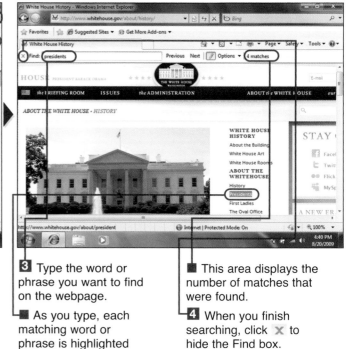

1 Click ▼ beside the search box. A menu appears.

2 Click **Find on this Page**.

■ The Find box appears.

3 Type the word or phrase you want to find on the webpage.

■ As you type, each matching word or phrase is highlighted on the webpage.

■ This area displays the number of matches that were found.

4 When you finish searching, click ✕ to hide the Find box.

You can browse the web without leaving any trace of your web activity in Internet Explorer.

For example, you may want to browse the web privately when shopping for a surprise gift on a family computer or checking e-mail at an Internet café.

When browsing the web privately, other people who use your computer will not see the websites you visit, the searches you perform and the usernames and passwords you enter.

Browsing the web privately does not prevent another person on your network, such as a network administrator, from viewing the websites you visit.

BROWSE THE WEB PRIVATELY

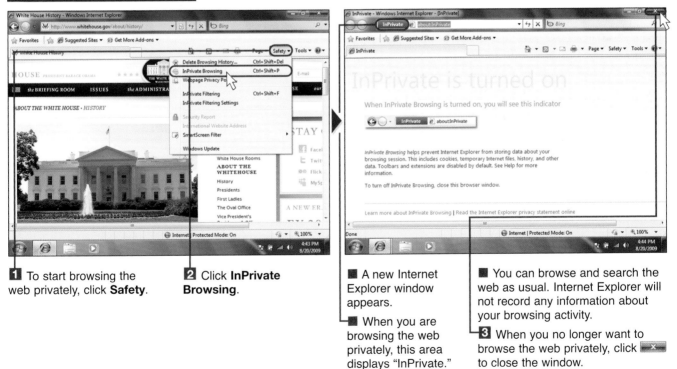

1 To start browsing the web privately, click **Safety**.

2 Click **InPrivate Browsing**.

■ A new Internet Explorer window appears.

■ When you are browsing the web privately, this area displays "InPrivate."

■ You can browse and search the web as usual. Internet Explorer will not record any information about your browsing activity.

3 When you no longer want to browse the web privately, click ▬✕▬ to close the window.

VIEW SUGGESTED SITES

When viewing a webpage, Internet Explorer can suggest similar websites that you might be interested in.

Internet Explorer suggests similar websites based on the webpages you have viewed.

VIEW SUGGESTED SITES

1 When you are viewing a webpage and want to see a list of similar websites that you might be interested in, click **Suggested Sites**.

■ A list of similar websites that you might be interested in appears.

2 To display a website in the list, click the website.

*Note: The Suggested Sites feature must be on to view the list of suggested websites. To turn the feature on, click **Tools** at the top-right corner of the Internet Explorer window and then click **Suggested Sites** on the menu that appears. In the confirmation dialog box that appears, click **Yes**.*

With Accelerators, you can select a word or phrase on a webpage and then choose from a variety of online services to instantly learn more about the text.

For example, you can select a word or phrase on a webpage and then instantly show a map, search the web, translate the text and more.

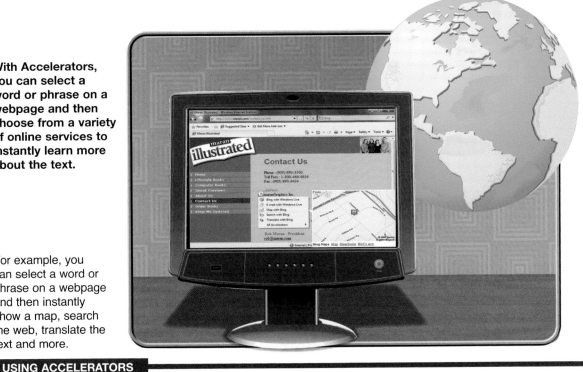

USING ACCELERATORS

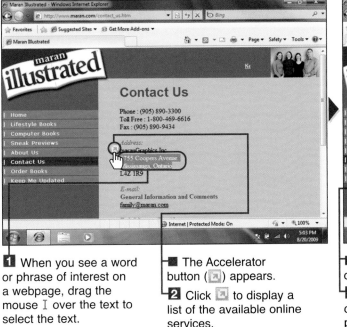

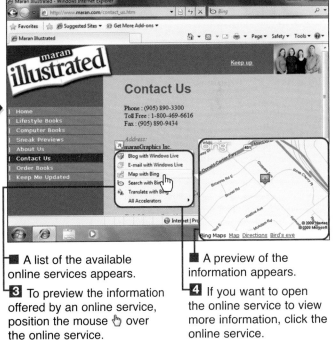

1 When you see a word or phrase of interest on a webpage, drag the mouse I over the text to select the text.

■ The Accelerator button ( ) appears.

2 Click to display a list of the available online services.

■ A list of the available online services appears.

3 To preview the information offered by an online service, position the mouse over the online service.

■ A preview of the information appears.

4 If you want to open the online service to view more information, click the online service.

ADD A WEB SLICE

With Web Slices, you can instantly see when updated content is available for your favorite webpages. For example, you can monitor webpage content such as weather reports, news headlines, sport scores, stock quotes and auction prices.

A Web Slice is a "slice" or part of a webpage that you can monitor.

Web Slices you add appear on the Favorites bar. For more information on the Favorites bar, see page 214.

ADD A WEB SLICE

■ When a Web Slice is available on a webpage, the Add Web Slices button (▨) appears in this area.

■ When you position the mouse ☟ over webpage content that is a Web Slice, ▨ also appears beside the content.

1 Click ▨ to add the Web Slice to the Favorites bar.

■ The Internet Explorer dialog box appears.

2 Click **Add to Favorites Bar** to add the Web Slice to the Favorites bar.

Tip

How do I remove a Web Slice from the Favorites bar?

If you no longer want a Web Slice to appear on the Favorites bar, right-click the button for the Web Slice and then click **Delete** on the menu that appears. In the confirmation dialog box that appears, click **Yes**.

Tip

Where can I see a list of available Web Slices?

You can visit the Internet Explorer Add-ons Gallery, located at www.ieaddons.com, to see a list of Web Slices that you can add. To quickly visit the Add-ons Gallery, click the **Get More Add-ons** button on the Favorites bar and then click ➔ in the preview window that appears.

VIEW WEB SLICE CONTENT

■ The Web Slice appears as a button on the Favorites bar.

■ When new content becomes available for a Web Slice, the button for the Web Slice appears **bold**.

1 To view the updated content for a Web Slice, click the button for the Web Slice on the Favorites bar.

■ A preview of the updated content appears.

2 If you want to open the webpage that offers the Web Slice, click ➔.

■ To close the preview, click the button for the Web Slice on the Favorites bar again.

Exchange E-Mail

START WINDOWS LIVE MAIL

You can start Windows
Live Mail to open and
read the contents of your
e-mail messages.

Windows Live Mail is not
included in Windows 7,
but the program is available
for free at the Windows
Live Essentials website
(http://download.live.com).
For more information on
this website, see page 50.

The first time you start
Windows Live Mail, a dialog
box will appear if you have not
yet set up an e-mail account.
Follow the instructions in the dialog
box to add an e-mail account.

START WINDOWS LIVE MAIL

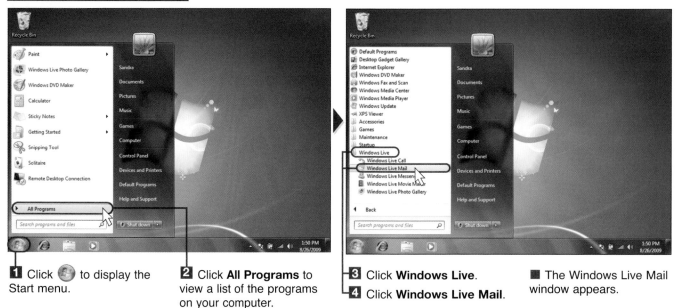

1 Click ● to display the
Start menu.

2 Click **All Programs** to
view a list of the programs
on your computer.

3 Click **Windows Live**.

4 Click **Windows Live Mail**.

■ The Windows Live Mail
window appears.

Tip

What folders are used to store my messages?

Inbox
Stores messages sent to you.

Drafts
Stores messages you have not yet completed.

Sent items
Stores copies of messages you have sent.

Junk e-mail
Stores junk messages sent to you.

Deleted items
Stores messages you have deleted.

 Tip

What are the Quick views folders?

Windows Live Mail provides three special Quick views folders that allow you to quickly view certain messages.

Unread e-mail
Displays all unread messages.

Unread from contacts
Displays all unread messages sent by people in your contacts list.

Unread feeds
Displays all unread messages from feeds you have subscribed to.

Note: Feeds, also known as RSS feeds or web feeds, offer frequently updated content published by websites. Feeds are often used by news and blog websites.

READ MESSAGES

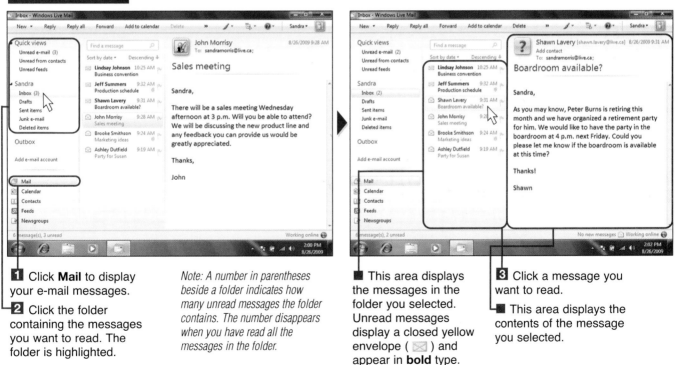

1 Click **Mail** to display your e-mail messages.

2 Click the folder containing the messages you want to read. The folder is highlighted.

Note: A number in parentheses beside a folder indicates how many unread messages the folder contains. The number disappears when you have read all the messages in the folder.

■ This area displays the messages in the folder you selected. Unread messages display a closed yellow envelope (✉) and appear in **bold** type.

3 Click a message you want to read.

■ This area displays the contents of the message you selected.

WORK WITH MESSAGES

When reading your messages, you can display a flag beside an important message to make the message stand out.

You can also mark a message as unread to help remind you to review the message again at a later time.

A staff meeting will be held in Conference Room A at 4:10 p.m. on each of the following days:
June 17th
July 7th
August 23rd
September 15th
All staff members must attend these meetings!

David Walker
President

If a message is a threat or may be a threat, a warning will appear in the message. For example, a phishing message is a message that may appear to be from a real company, but will send you to a fake website or scam you into providing personal information.

FLAG A MESSAGE

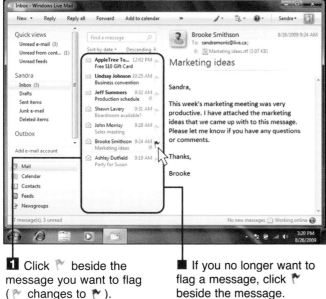

1 Click 🏳 beside the message you want to flag (🏳 changes to 🚩).

■ If you no longer want to flag a message, click 🚩 beside the message.

MARK A MESSAGE AS UNREAD

■ Messages you have read display an open envelope (✉) and appear in regular type.

1 Right-click the message you want to mark as unread. A menu appears.

2 Click **Mark as unread**.

Can I view a message in a larger area?

Yes. If you want to view a message in a larger area, double-click the message. The message will appear in a separate window. When you finish reading the message, click ██X██ to close the window.

How do I print a message?

To print a message, right-click the message you want to print and then click **Print** on the menu that appears. In the Print dialog box, click **Print** to print the message.

VIEW BLOCKED CONTENT

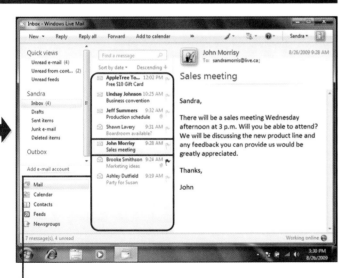

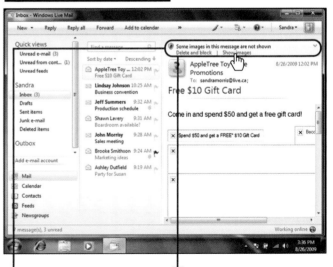

■ The message appears unread. Unread messages display a closed envelope (⊠) and appear in **bold** type.

■ If you want to once again display a message as read, repeat steps **1** and **2**, except select **Mark as read** in step **2**.

■ If Windows Live Mail considers a message to be a threat or a possible threat, a warning appears at the top of the message.

1 If the message is from a reliable source and you want to view the blocked content, click the option that allows you to unblock the content.

SEND A MESSAGE

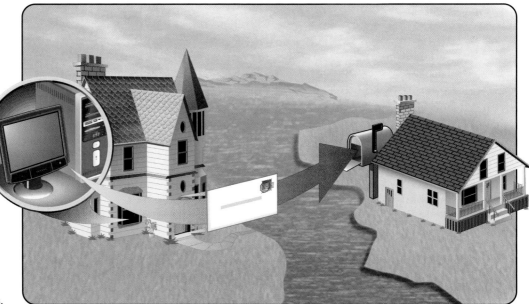

You can quickly and easily send an e-mail message to a friend, family member or colleague.

Sending a message written in CAPITAL LETTERS is annoying and difficult to read. This is called shouting. Always use uppercase and lowercase letters when typing messages.

SEND A MESSAGE

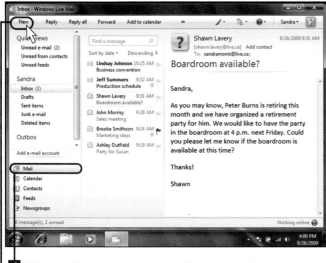

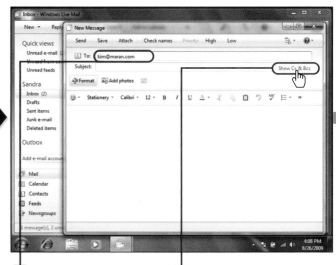

1 Click **Mail** to display your e-mail messages.

2 Click **New** to send a new message.

■ The New Message window appears.

3 Type the e-mail address of the person you want to receive the message.

Note: To send the message to more than one person, separate each e-mail address with a semicolon (;).

4 If you want to send a carbon copy or blind carbon copy of the message to another person, click **Show Cc & Bcc**.

Tip

When sending a message, what types of copies can I send?

When sending a message, you can send a carbon copy of a message or a blind carbon copy of a message.

Carbon copy (Cc)
Sends a copy of a message to a person who is not directly involved, but would be interested in the message.

Blind carbon copy (Bcc)
Sends a copy of a message to a person without anyone else knowing that the person received the message.

Tip

Can I send decorative e-mail messages?

Yes. Windows Live Mail includes several stationery designs that you can use to enhance your e-mail messages. When sending a message, click **Stationery** and then click **More stationery** on the menu that appears. In the dialog box that appears, click the stationery you want to use, such as Bubbles, Garden or Money, and then click **OK** to select the stationery.

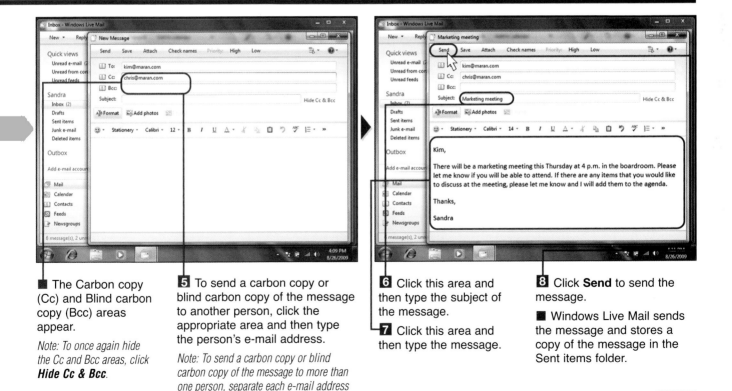

■ The Carbon copy (Cc) and Blind carbon copy (Bcc) areas appear.

Note: To once again hide the Cc and Bcc areas, click **Hide Cc & Bcc**.

5 To send a carbon copy or blind carbon copy of the message to another person, click the appropriate area and then type the person's e-mail address.

Note: To send a carbon copy or blind carbon copy of the message to more than one person, separate each e-mail address with a semicolon (;).

6 Click this area and then type the subject of the message.

7 Click this area and then type the message.

8 Click **Send** to send the message.

■ Windows Live Mail sends the message and stores a copy of the message in the Sent items folder.

CHECK SPELLING IN A MESSAGE

Before sending a message, you can correct all the spelling errors in the message.

Windows Live Mail compares every word in your message to words in its dictionary. If a word does not exist in the dictionary, the word is considered misspelled.

Windows Live Mail will not find a correctly spelled word used in the wrong context, such as "We have been in business for **sit** years." You should carefully review your message to find this type of error.

CHECK SPELLING IN A MESSAGE

■ Windows Live Mail displays a wavy red line below misspelled words. The wavy red lines will not appear when the person receives your message.

1 To correct the misspelled words in your message, click ABC .

■ The Spelling dialog box appears if Windows Live Mail finds a misspelled word in your message.

■ This area displays the first misspelled word.

■ This area displays suggestions for correcting the misspelled word.

Tip

Can Windows Live Mail automatically correct my spelling mistakes?

Yes. Windows Live Mail automatically corrects common spelling mistakes as you type. Here are a few examples.

adn	⟶	and
alot	⟶	a lot
comittee	⟶	committee
don;t	⟶	don't
nwe	⟶	new
occurence	⟶	occurrence
recieve	⟶	receive
seperate	⟶	separate
teh	⟶	the

Tip

How can I quickly correct a misspelled word?

To quickly correct a misspelled word in your message, right-click the word. A menu will appear with suggestions to correct the word. Click the suggestion you want to use to correct the word.

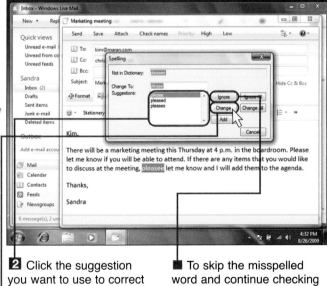

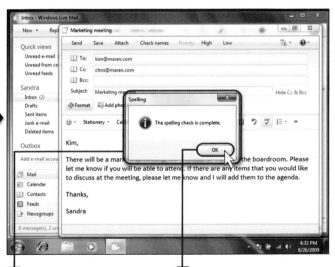

2 Click the suggestion you want to use to correct the misspelled word.

3 Click **Change** to correct the misspelled word in your message.

■ To skip the misspelled word and continue checking your message, click **Ignore**.

*Note: To skip the misspelled word and all other occurrences of the misspelled word in your message, click **Ignore All**.*

4 Correct or ignore misspelled words until a dialog box appears, telling you the spelling check is complete.

5 Click **OK** to close the dialog box.

ADD PHOTOS TO A MESSAGE

You can add photos to a message you are sending so you can share the photos with your friends and family.

ADD PHOTOS TO A MESSAGE

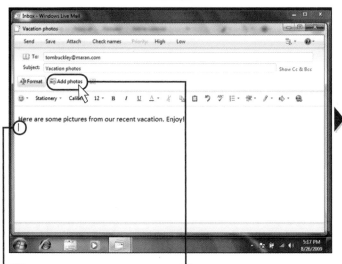

1 To create a message, perform steps **1** to **7** starting on page 228.

2 Click the location in the message where you want to add photos.

3 Click **Add photos** to add photos to the message.

■ The Add Photos dialog box appears.

■ This area shows the location of the displayed photos. You can click this area to select a different location.

4 Click a photo you want to add to the message.

5 Click **Add** to add the photo to the message.

Will photos I add to a message be available on the Internet?

If you are signed in to Windows Live Mail with a Windows Live ID, high-quality versions of the photos you add to a message will be placed on the Internet when you send the message. When a person receives the message, they can view the high-quality photos in an online slideshow. The message will display smaller versions of the photos so the message transfers faster.

Note: A Windows Live ID is the e-mail address and password you use to sign in to Windows Live programs and services, such as Windows Live Hotmail.

How do I send a file with a message?

To send a document, spreadsheet, video, or other type of file with a message, create your message and then click **Attach** at the top of the window. In the dialog box that appears, click the file you want to attach and then click **Open**. The name and size of the file you select will appear below the Subject area in the message.

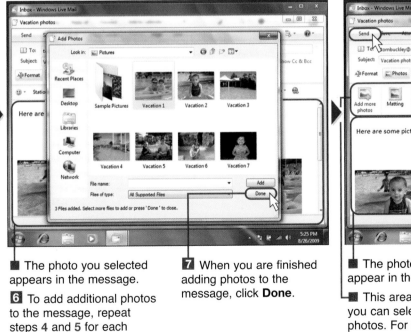

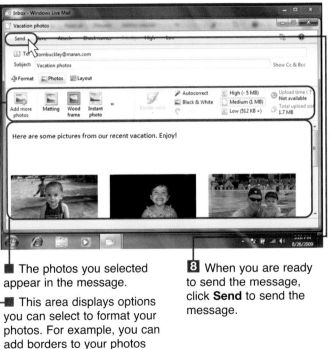

■ The photo you selected appears in the message.

6 To add additional photos to the message, repeat steps **4** and **5** for each photo you want to add.

7 When you are finished adding photos to the message, click **Done**.

■ The photos you selected appear in the message.

■ This area displays options you can select to format your photos. For example, you can add borders to your photos and change your photos to black and white.

8 When you are ready to send the message, click **Send** to send the message.

REPLY TO A MESSAGE

You can reply to a message to answer a question, express an opinion or supply additional information.

REPLY TO A MESSAGE

1 Click the message you want to reply to.

2 Click the reply option you want to use.

Reply
Sends a reply to only the author.

Reply all
Sends a reply to the author and everyone who received the original message.

■ A window appears for you to compose your reply.

■ Windows Live Mail fills in the e-mail address(es) for you.

■ Windows Live Mail also fills in the subject, starting the subject with **Re:**.

Tip

Can I format the text in my messages?

Yes. To format the text in a message, you first need to select the text you want to format by dragging the mouse I over the text. You can then perform one of the following common formatting tasks.

✓ To change the font of text, click the Font button and then select the font you want to use from the list of fonts that appears.

✓ To change the size of text, click the Font size button and then select the font size you want to use from the list of sizes that appears.

✓ To bold, italicize or underline text, click the Bold (**B**), Italic (*I*) or Underline (U) button.

✓ To color text, click △ and then select the color you want to use from the list of colors that appears.

■ Windows Live Mail includes a copy of the original message to help the reader identify which message you are replying to. This is called quoting.

3 Click this area and then type your reply.

4 Click **Send** to send the reply.

■ Windows Live Mail stores a copy of the message in the Sent items folder.

Note: The icon beside the original message changes from ✉ to ⬗ to indicate that you have replied to the message.

FORWARD A MESSAGE

After reading a message, you can add comments and then forward the message to a friend, family member or colleague.

Forwarding a message is useful when you know another person would be interested in a message.

FORWARD A MESSAGE

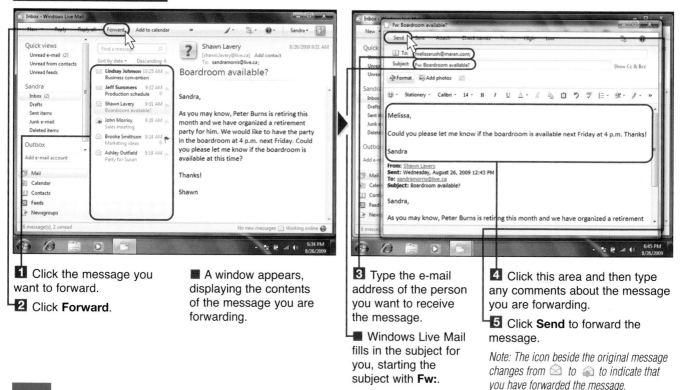

1 Click the message you want to forward.

2 Click **Forward**.

■ A window appears, displaying the contents of the message you are forwarding.

3 Type the e-mail address of the person you want to receive the message.

■ Windows Live Mail fills in the subject for you, starting the subject with **Fw:**.

4 Click this area and then type any comments about the message you are forwarding.

5 Click **Send** to forward the message.

Note: The icon beside the original message changes from ✉ to ⤷ to indicate that you have forwarded the message.

236

You can delete a
message you no
longer need.
Deleting messages
prevents your folders
from becoming
cluttered with
messages.

DELETE A MESSAGE

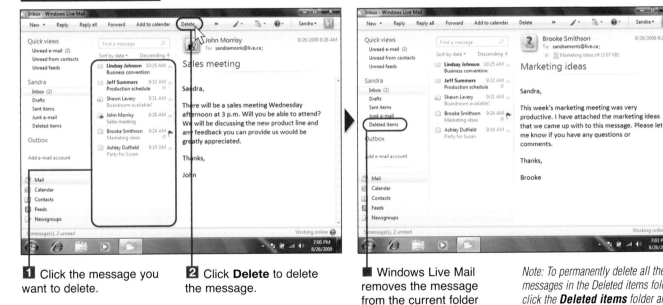

1 Click the message you
want to delete.

2 Click **Delete** to delete
the message.

■ Windows Live Mail
removes the message
from the current folder
and places the message
in the Deleted items
folder.

*Note: To permanently delete all the
messages in the Deleted items folder,
click the **Deleted items** folder and
then click* ✕ *beside the folder. In
the confirmation dialog box that
appears, click **Yes**.*

OPEN AN ATTACHED FILE

You can easily open a file attached to a message you receive.

Before opening an attached file, make sure the file is from a person you trust. Some files can contain a virus, which can damage the information on your computer. You can use an antivirus program to help protect your computer from viruses.

OPEN AN ATTACHED FILE

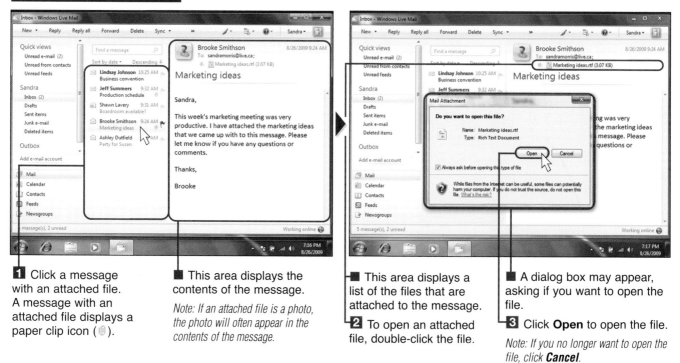

1 Click a message with an attached file. A message with an attached file displays a paper clip icon (📎).

■ This area displays the contents of the message.

Note: If an attached file is a photo, the photo will often appear in the contents of the message.

■ This area displays a list of the files that are attached to the message.

2 To open an attached file, double-click the file.

■ A dialog box may appear, asking if you want to open the file.

3 Click **Open** to open the file.

*Note: If you no longer want to open the file, click **Cancel**.*

If you are waiting for an important message, you can have Windows Live Mail immediately check for new messages.

You can also change how often Windows Live Mail checks for new messages. Windows Live Mail initially checks for new messages every 30 minutes when you are connected to the Internet.

CHECK FOR NEW MESSAGES

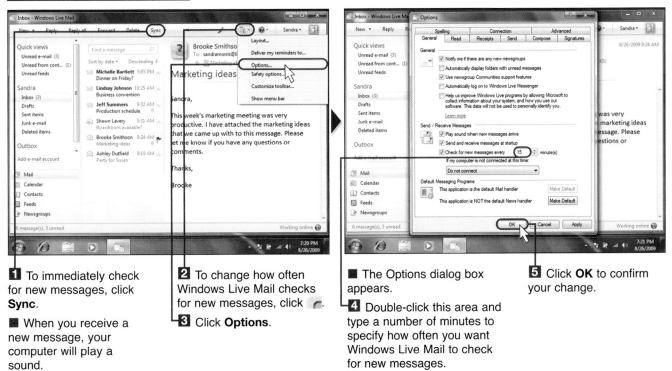

1 To immediately check for new messages, click **Sync**.

■ When you receive a new message, your computer will play a sound.

2 To change how often Windows Live Mail checks for new messages, click 🔻.

3 Click **Options**.

■ The Options dialog box appears.

4 Double-click this area and type a number of minutes to specify how often you want Windows Live Mail to check for new messages.

5 Click **OK** to confirm your change.

You can add contacts to store e-mail addresses and other information about friends, family members and clients, including phone numbers, addresses and birthdays.

When you send an e-mail message, you can select a contact to have Windows Live Mail quickly fill in the e-mail address of the person for you.

ADD A CONTACT

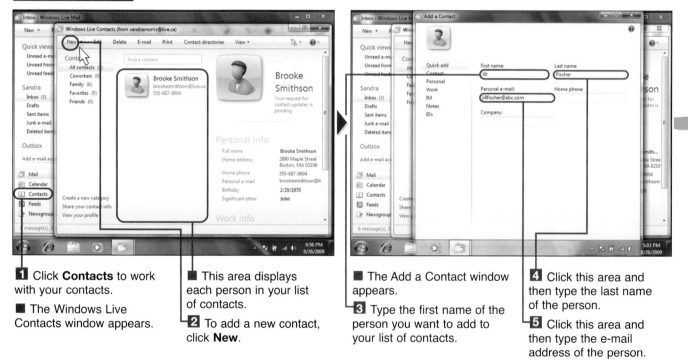

1 Click **Contacts** to work with your contacts.

■ The Windows Live Contacts window appears.

■ This area displays each person in your list of contacts.

2 To add a new contact, click **New**.

■ The Add a Contact window appears.

3 Type the first name of the person you want to add to your list of contacts.

4 Click this area and then type the last name of the person.

5 Click this area and then type the e-mail address of the person.

Tip

Is there a faster way to add a contact?

Yes. When you receive a message from a person you want to add to your list of contacts, click **Add contact** at the top of the message. In the Add a Contact window that appears, Windows Live Mail will enter the name and e-mail address of the person for you. To add the contact to your list of contacts, click **Add contact**.

Tip

How do I change the information for a contact?

To change the information for a contact, click **Contacts** at the left side of the Windows Live Mail window. In your list of contacts that appears, double-click the contact you want to change. Click the category for the information you want to change and then make the necessary changes. When you finish making your changes, click **Save**.

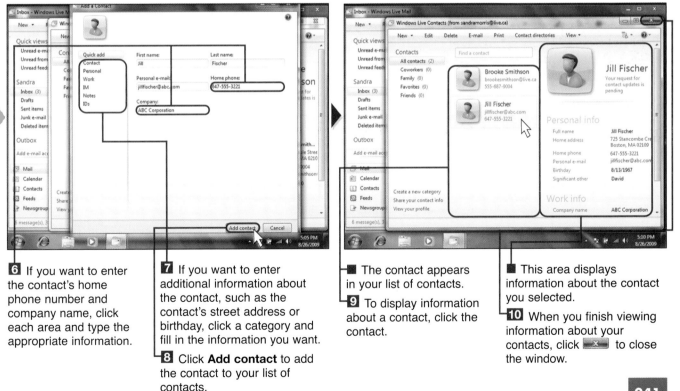

6 If you want to enter the contact's home phone number and company name, click each area and type the appropriate information.

7 If you want to enter additional information about the contact, such as the contact's street address or birthday, click a category and fill in the information you want.

8 Click **Add contact** to add the contact to your list of contacts.

■ The contact appears in your list of contacts.

9 To display information about a contact, click the contact.

■ This area displays information about the contact you selected.

10 When you finish viewing information about your contacts, click ☒ to close the window.

When sending a message, you can select the name of the person you want to receive the message from your list of contacts.

Selecting names from your list of contacts saves you from having to remember the e-mail addresses of people you often send messages to.

SEND A MESSAGE TO A CONTACT

1 Click **Mail** to display your e-mail messages.

2 Click **New** to send a new message.

■ The New Message window appears.

3 To select a name from your list of contacts, click **To:**.

■ The Send an E-mail window appears.

4 Click the name of the person you want to receive the message.

5 Click **To**.

■ This area displays the name of the person you selected.

■ You can repeat steps 4 and 5 for each person you want to receive the message.

Tip

How can I address a message I want to send?

To
Sends the message to the person you specify.

Carbon copy (Cc)
Sends a copy of the message to a person who is not directly involved, but would be interested in the message.

Blind carbon copy (Bcc)
Sends a copy of the message to a person without anyone else knowing that the person received the message.

Tip

Is there a faster way to select a name from my list of contacts?

Yes. When sending a message, you can quickly select a name from your list of contacts by typing the first few letters of a person's name or e-mail address in the To:, Cc: or Bcc: area in the New Message window. As you type, a list of matching contacts will appear. Click the name of the person you want to receive the message.

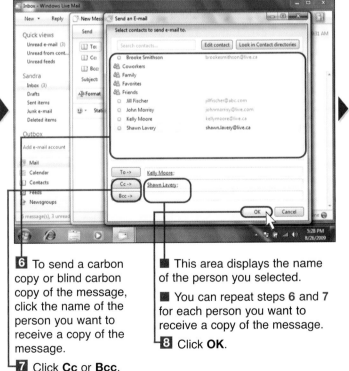

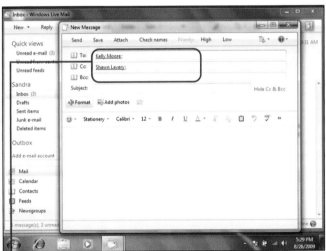

6 To send a carbon copy or blind carbon copy of the message, click the name of the person you want to receive a copy of the message.

7 Click **Cc** or **Bcc**.

■ This area displays the name of the person you selected.

■ You can repeat steps **6** and **7** for each person you want to receive a copy of the message.

8 Click **OK**.

■ This area displays the name of each person you selected.

■ You can now finish composing the message.

Note: To finish composing a message, perform steps 6 to 8 on page 229.

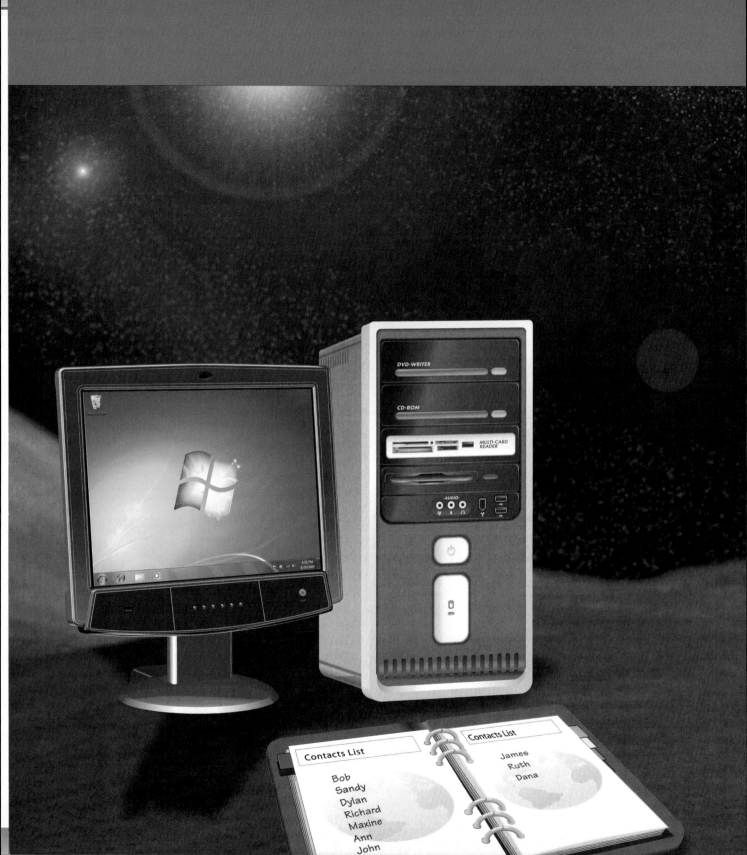

DVD-WRITER

CD-ROM

MULTI-CARD
READER

-AUDIO-

Contacts List

Contacts List

Bob
Sandy
Dylan
Richard
Maxine
Ann
John

James
Ruth
Dana

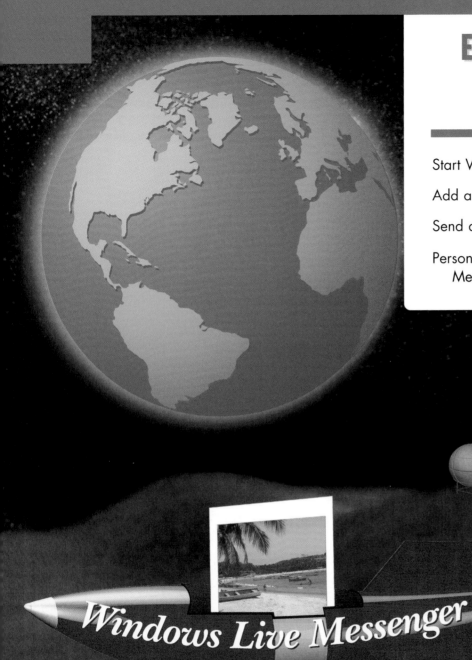

Exchange Instant Messages

Windows Live Messenger

START WINDOWS LIVE MESSENGER

You can use Windows Live Messenger to exchange instant messages with friends, family and coworkers.

Windows Live Messenger is not included in Windows 7, but the program is available for free at the Windows Live Essentials website (http://download.live.com). For more information on this website, see page 50.

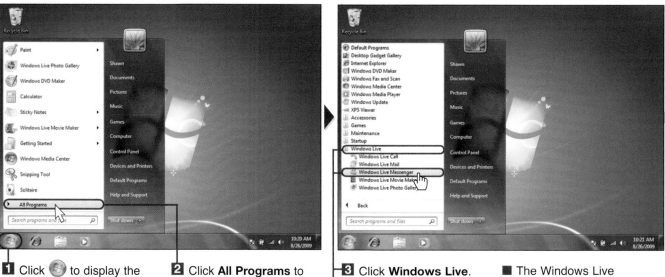

1 Click ⊕ to display the Start menu.

2 Click **All Programs** to view a list of the programs on your computer.

3 Click **Windows Live**.

4 Click **Windows Live Messenger**.

■ The Windows Live Messenger sign in window appears.

Tip

Can Windows Live Messenger sign me in automatically?

Yes. After you type your Windows Live e-mail address and password, click the box ( ) beside **Remember me**, **Remember my password** and **Sign me in automatically** to add a check mark ( ) to each box. Windows Live Messenger will now remember your e-mail address and password and sign you in automatically each time you start Windows Live Messenger.

Tip

How do I sign out of Windows Live Messenger?

When you finish using Windows Live Messenger, click your name at the top of the window and then click **Sign out from here** on the menu that appears. You can click ✕ at the top of the Windows Live Messenger window to close the window. To once again display the Windows Live Messenger window at any time, click its icon ( ) on the taskbar.

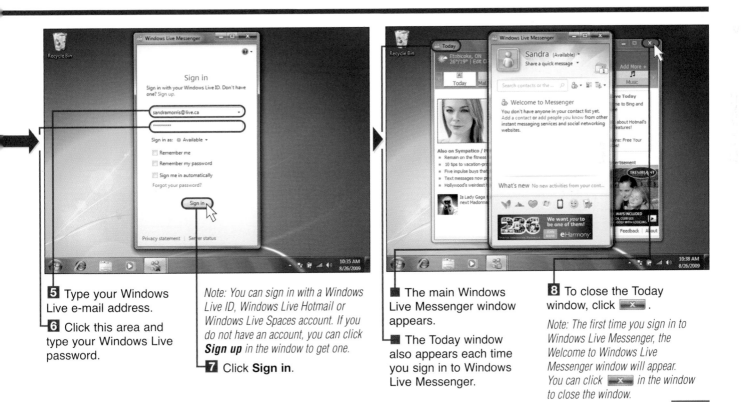

5 Type your Windows Live e-mail address.

6 Click this area and type your Windows Live password.

Note: You can sign in with a Windows Live ID, Windows Live Hotmail or Windows Live Spaces account. If you do not have an account, you can click Sign up in the window to get one.

7 Click **Sign in**.

■ The main Windows Live Messenger window appears.

■ The Today window also appears each time you sign in to Windows Live Messenger.

8 To close the Today window, click ✕ .

Note: The first time you sign in to Windows Live Messenger, the Welcome to Windows Live Messenger window will appear. You can click ✕ in the window to close the window.

You can add your friends, family and coworkers to your contacts list so you can exchange instant messages with them.

ADD A CONTACT

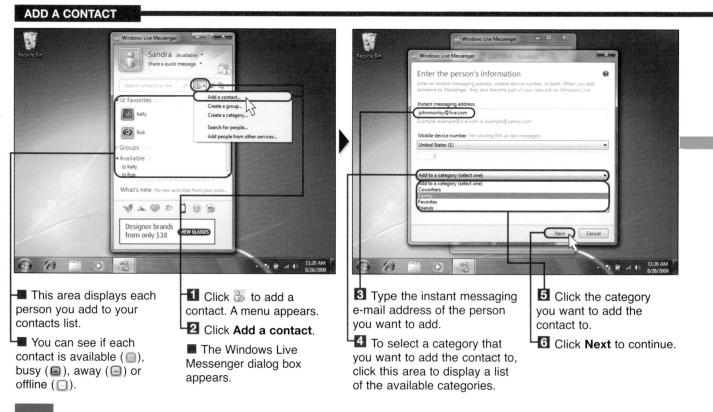

■ This area displays each person you add to your contacts list.

■ You can see if each contact is available (■), busy (■), away (■) or offline (□).

1 Click 🔲 to add a contact. A menu appears.

2 Click **Add a contact**.

■ The Windows Live Messenger dialog box appears.

3 Type the instant messaging e-mail address of the person you want to add.

4 To select a category that you want to add the contact to, click this area to display a list of the available categories.

5 Click the category you want to add the contact to.

6 Click **Next** to continue.

Tip

When adding a contact, can I enter a person's mobile device number?

Yes. You can enter a person's mobile device number so you can send them text messages. When adding a contact, click the area below **Mobile device number** and then select the person's country from the list that appears. Then click in the empty box below the country and type the person's mobile device number.

Note: When adding a contact, you can enter an instant messaging e-mail address, a mobile device number or both.

Tip

How do I remove a contact from my contacts list?

If you no longer exchange instant messages with a person in your contacts list, you can remove them from the list. In the Windows Live Messenger window, right-click the contact you want to remove and then click **Delete contact** on the menu that appears. In the confirmation dialog box that appears, click **Delete contact**.

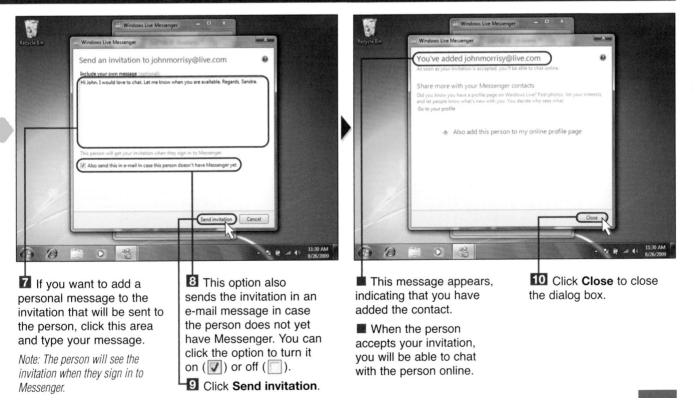

7 If you want to add a personal message to the invitation that will be sent to the person, click this area and type your message.

Note: The person will see the invitation when they sign in to Messenger.

8 This option also sends the invitation in an e-mail message in case the person does not yet have Messenger. You can click the option to turn it on (☑) or off (☐).

9 Click **Send invitation**.

■ This message appears, indicating that you have added the contact.

■ When the person accepts your invitation, you will be able to chat with the person online.

10 Click **Close** to close the dialog box.

251

SEND AN INSTANT MESSAGE

You can send an instant message to a person in your contacts list.

For information on adding a person to your contacts list, see page 250.

If you send an instant message to a person that is offline, they will receive your message the next time they sign in to Windows Live Messenger.

SEND AN INSTANT MESSAGE

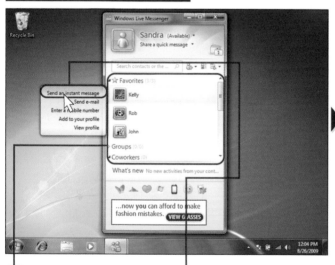

1 Click the contact you want to send an instant message to. A menu appears.

2 Click **Send an instant message**.

■ A conversation window appears.

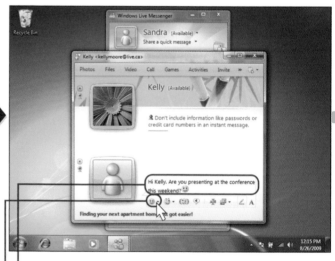

3 Type the message you want to send.

4 If you want to add an emoticon to your message to express an emotion, click 😃 to display the available emoticons. Then click the emoticon you want to add, such as 😃, 😎 or 😦.

5 When you are ready to send the message, press the Enter key.

Tip

Can I share photos during an instant message conversation?

Yes. In the conversation window, click **Photos** and then click the photo you want to share in the dialog box that appears. Click **Open** to add the photo to the conversation window. To share another photo, click **Add**. If more than one photo has been added to the window, move the mouse ⌖ over the displayed photo and then click ⏮ or ⏭ to flip through the photos.

Note: If you want to stop sharing photos, click × in the conversation window. If another person is using a version of Messenger that cannot share photos, you will not be able to share photos with the person.

Tip

How do I send a message to a mobile device?

To send a text message to a mobile device, click the contact you want to send a message to and then click **Send mobile text (SMS)** on the menu that appears. A dialog box will appear, stating that the person may be charged for the message you send. Click **OK** to close the dialog box. Type the message you want to send and then press the Enter key.

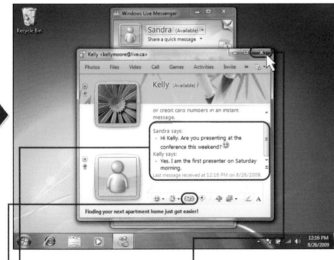

RECEIVE AN INSTANT MESSAGE

■ This area displays the message you sent and the ongoing conversation.

6 If the other person is taking a long time to respond, you can click 😊 to shake the conversation window to get their attention.

7 When you finish exchanging messages with the other person, click ✖ to close the window.

*Note: The first time you close the conversation window, Windows asks if you want to save all of your conversations. Click **Yes** or **No** and then click **OK**.*

■ When you receive an instant message that is not part of an ongoing conversation, your computer makes a sound and briefly displays a box containing the message.

1 To display the conversation window so you can reply to the message, click inside the box.

Note: You can also click 🖥 on the taskbar and then click the conversation window to display the window.

PERSONALIZE WINDOWS LIVE MESSENGER

You can change your status to let other people know that you are currently not available.

If you do not use your computer for more than five minutes, your status automatically changes to Away. When you resume using your computer, your status will return to Available.

With Windows Live Messenger, you can also add a personal message that your contacts can see. You can also add frequently used contacts to your list of favorites.

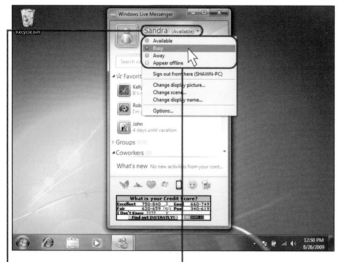

■ Your status appears beside your name.

1 If you want to change your status, click your name. A menu appears.

2 Click the status you want other people to see.

■ When you change your status, other people can still send you instant messages.

1 If you want to add a personal message that your contacts can see, click this area and type your personal message. Then press the Enter key.

■ If a contact has added a personal message, you will see the message beside their name in the contacts list.

Note: To remove your personal message, click your current message and then press the Delete key. Then press the Enter key.

Tip

Can my personal message show what song I am listening to?

Yes. If you want your personal message to show the song you are currently listening to, click ▼ below your name in the Windows Live Messenger window and then click **Show what I'm listening to** on the menu that appears. You can repeat these steps to turn this feature off.

Note: This feature only works when you are using Windows Media Player or Apple iTunes to play your music.

Tip

How do I remove a contact from my Favorites list?

If you no longer want a contact to appear in your Favorites list, right-click the contact in your Favorites list. On the menu that appears, click **Remove from favorites**. The contact will disappear from your Favorites list, but will still appear in its original category.

ADD A CONTACT TO FAVORITES

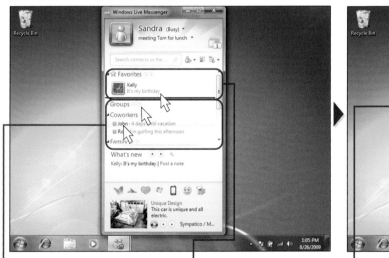

■ If you often send messages to a person in your contacts list, you may want to add the person to your Favorites list.

1 To add a contact to your Favorites list, position the mouse ▷ over the contact.

2 Drag the contact to your Favorites list.

■ A black line shows where the contact will appear.

■ The contact appears in your Favorites list.

■ The contact also still appears in its original category.

CONTINUED

When using Windows Live Messenger, you can change the picture that appears beside your name.

You can also change the scene, or background picture, that appears at the top of your main Windows Live Messenger window.

CHANGE YOUR PICTURE

■ In your Favorites list, you can see the picture that each contact has selected.

■ This area displays your picture.

1 To change your picture, click your picture.

■ The Display Picture dialog box appears.

2 Click the picture you want to use.

3 Click **OK** to change your picture.

Tip

Will other people see the picture and scene I select?

Yes. When you chat with a friend, family member or co-worker, the picture and scene you select will appear in their conversation window. You will see the picture and scene the other person selected in your conversation window.

Tip

Can I use an image on my computer for my picture or scene?

Yes. If you want to use an image on your computer for your picture or scene, click **Browse** in the Display Picture or Scene dialog box. Click the image you want to use in the dialog box that appears and then click **Open**. Then click **OK**.

CHANGE YOUR SCENE

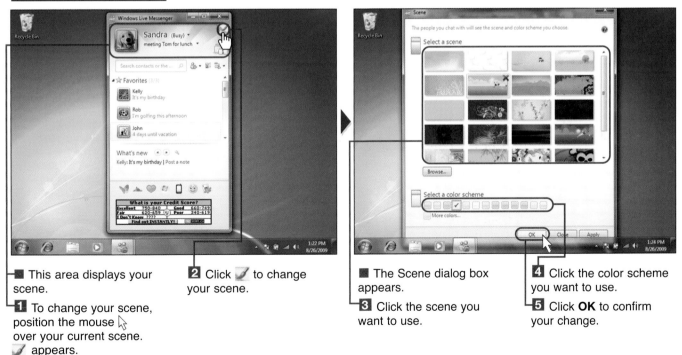

■ This area displays your scene.

1 To change your scene, position the mouse ▷ over your current scene. ✍ appears.

2 Click ✍ to change your scene.

■ The Scene dialog box appears.

3 Click the scene you want to use.

4 Click the color scheme you want to use.

5 Click **OK** to confirm your change.

Work on a Network

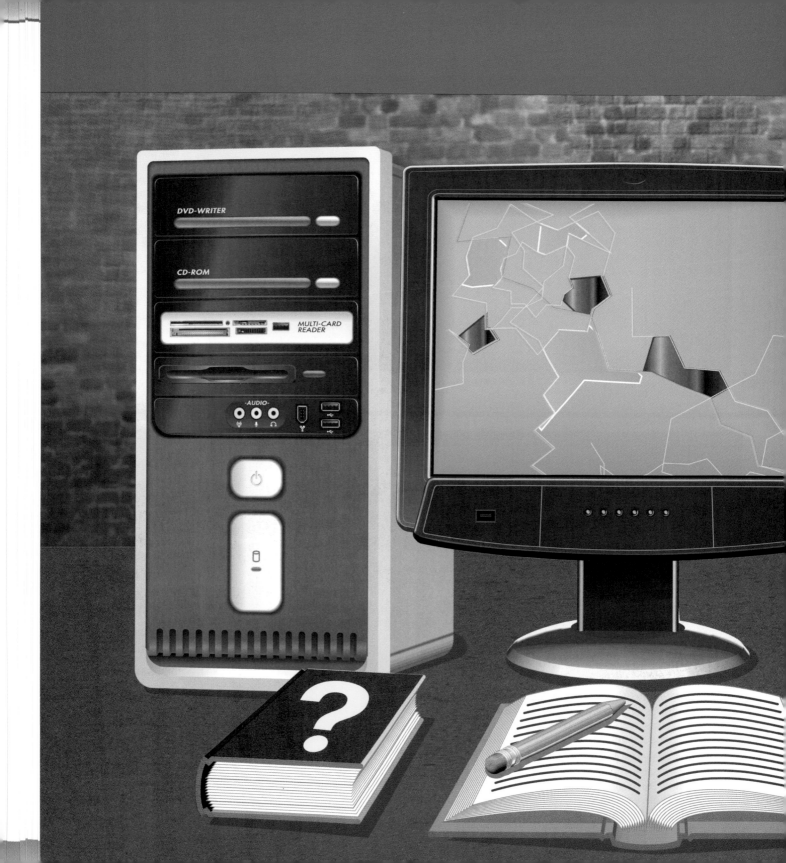

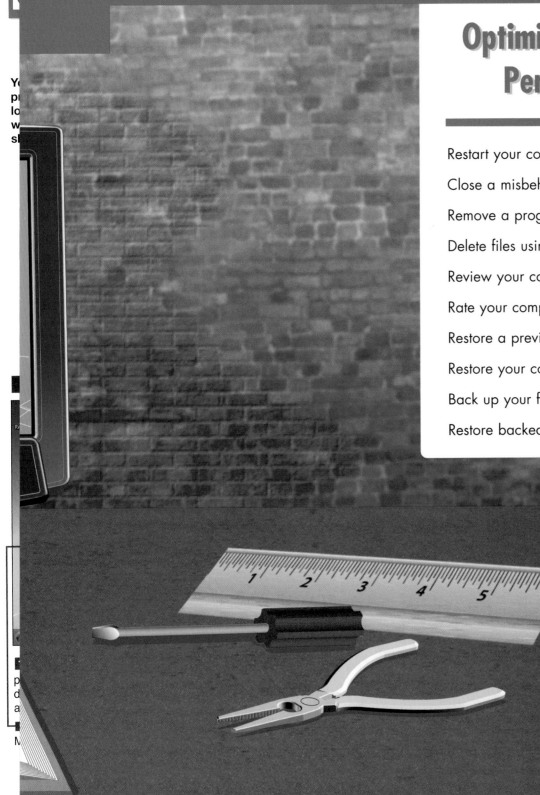

Optimize Computer Performance

Disk Cleanup can show you exactly how much space you can free up on your computer by removing unnecessary files.

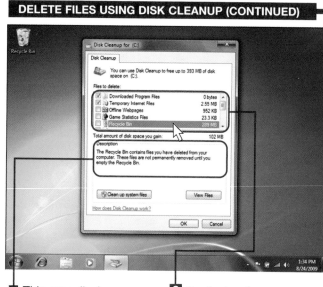

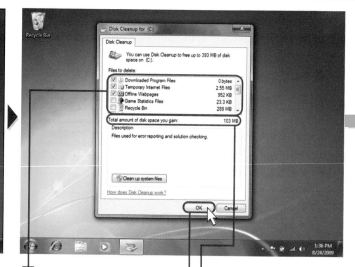

■ This area displays a description of the highlighted file type.

8 To display the description for a different file type, click the file type.

9 Windows will delete the files for each file type that displays a check mark (☑). Click the box (☐) beside a file type to add or remove a check mark.

■ This area displays the total disk space Windows will free up by deleting the types of files you selected.

10 When you finish selecting the types of files you want to delete, click **OK** to delete the files.

Tip

Can I see which files Disk Cleanup will remove?

Yes. Before Disk Cleanup removes unnecessary files from your computer, you can see which files will be removed. In the Disk Cleanup dialog box, select a file type of interest and then click the **View Files** button. A window will appear, displaying the files that Disk Cleanup will remove. The View Files button is not available for some file types.

Tip

Are there other ways I can remove unnecessary files from my computer?

Yes. Programs you no longer use and files you no longer need take up valuable disk space on your computer. You can remove unnecessary programs and files to free up disk space. For more information, see page 280 to remove programs and page 69 to delete files.

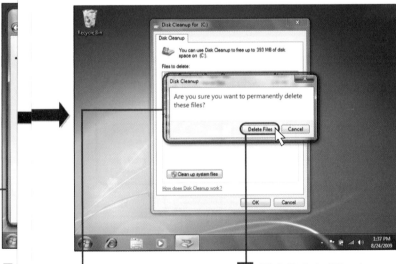

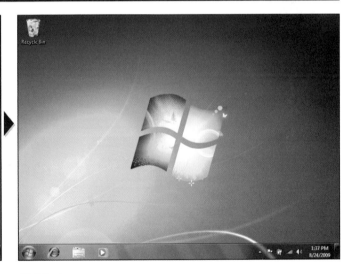

■ A dialog box appears, confirming that you want to delete the files.

11 Click **Delete Files** to permanently delete the files.

■ Windows removes the unnecessary files from your computer.

RESTORE YOUR COMPUTER

You
that
ove
of y
This
as t
Exp
bas
bas

The
on t
diffe
com
proc
gene
gam
hard

If you are experiencing problems with your computer, you can use the System Restore feature to return your computer to a time before the problems occurred.

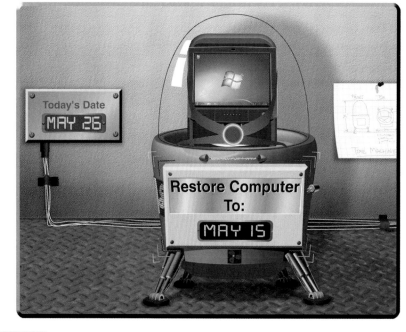

For example, if your computer does not work properly after you install a program, you can restore your computer to a time before you installed the program.

RESTORE YOUR COMPUTER

■ Before restoring your computer to an earlier time, you should close all open files and programs.

1 Click 🏁 to display the Start menu.

2 Click **All Programs** to view a list of the programs on your computer.

3 Click **Accessories**.

4 Click **System Tools**.

Tip

How does System Restore work?

System Restore uses restore points to return your computer to a time before any problems occurred. A restore point is an earlier time that you can return your computer to. Windows automatically creates restore points every week and just before an important change is made to your computer, such as before you install a new program.

Tip

Will I need to re-install any programs after restoring my computer?

When you restore your computer to an earlier time, any programs you added after that date are deleted. Files you created using the program will not be deleted, but you may need to re-install the program to work with the files again.

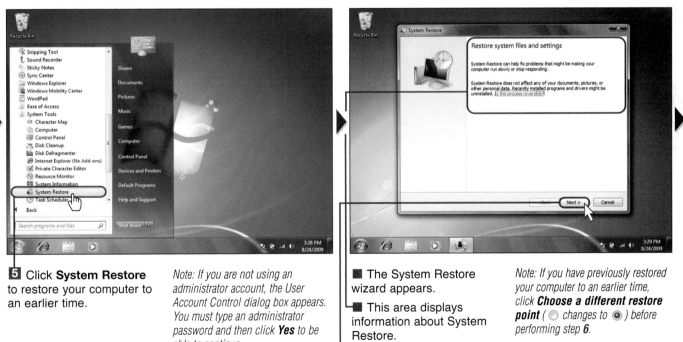

5 Click **System Restore** to restore your computer to an earlier time.

Note: If you are not using an administrator account, the User Account Control dialog box appears. You must type an administrator password and then click Yes to be able to continue.

■ The System Restore wizard appears.

■ This area displays information about System Restore.

6 Click **Next** to continue.

*Note: If you have previously restored your computer to an earlier time, click **Choose a different restore point** (○ changes to ●) before performing step 6.*

CONTINUED

RESTORE YOUR COMPUTER

When you restore your computer to an earlier time, you will not lose any of your personal files, such as your documents, photos or e-mail messages.

Since System Restore does not affect your personal files, System Restore cannot help you recover lost, deleted or damaged files.

RESTORE YOUR COMPUTER (CONTINUED)

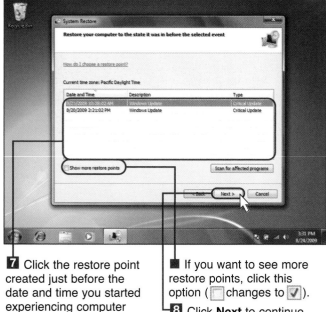

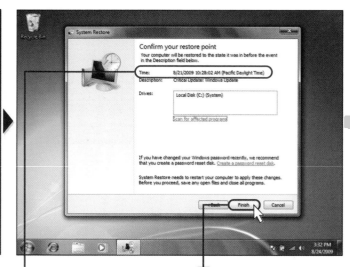

7 Click the restore point created just before the date and time you started experiencing computer problems.

■ If you want to see more restore points, click this option (☐ changes to ☑).

8 Click **Next** to continue.

■ This area displays the date and time your computer will be restored to.

9 Click **Finish** to restore your computer.

Tip

Before I restore my computer, can I see what programs will be affected?

Yes. After you select a restore point in step 7 below, click the **Scan for affected programs** button. A dialog box will appear, showing you a list of the programs and drivers that will be deleted and a list of the programs and drivers that might be restored on your computer. When you finish reviewing the information, click **Close**.

Note: A driver is software that allows a device, such as a printer or mouse, to work with your computer.

Tip

Can I reverse the changes made when I restored my computer to an earlier time?

Yes. Any changes that the System Restore feature makes to your computer are completely reversible. To undo your last restoration, perform steps **1** to **5** starting on page 292 to display the System Restore wizard. Click **Undo System Restore** (○ changes to ◉) and then click **Next** to continue. Click **Finish** to start the restore process.

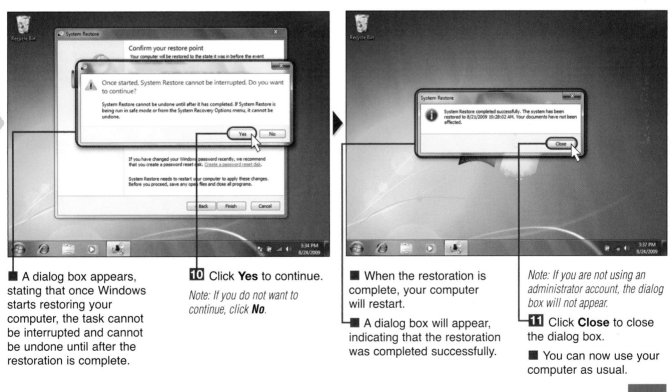

■ A dialog box appears, stating that once Windows starts restoring your computer, the task cannot be interrupted and cannot be undone until after the restoration is complete.

10 Click **Yes** to continue.

*Note: If you do not want to continue, click **No**.*

■ When the restoration is complete, your computer will restart.

■ A dialog box will appear, indicating that the restoration was completed successfully.

Note: If you are not using an administrator account, the dialog box will not appear.

11 Click **Close** to close the dialog box.

■ You can now use your computer as usual.

BACK UP YOUR FILES

You should back up the files on your computer to a storage device, such as an external hard drive. This will provide you with extra copies of your files in case of fire, theft or computer failure.

You can back up your files to an external hard drive, USB flash drive, CD or DVD. Microsoft recommends that you back up your files to an external hard drive.

When backing up files to an external hard drive, Windows can save a system image, which you can use to restore the contents of your computer if it stops working. When backing up files, you cannot save a system image on a USB flash drive, CD or DVD.

BACK UP YOUR FILES

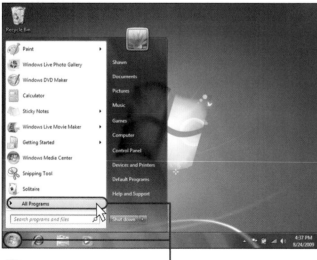

1 Connect an external hard drive to your computer.

■ Instead, you can connect a USB flash drive or insert a recordable CD or DVD into your computer's drive.

Note: If the AutoPlay window appears, click [x] *to close the window.*

2 Click [●] to display the Start menu.

3 Click **All Programs**.

4 Click **Maintenance**.

5 Click **Backup and Restore**.

■ The Backup and Restore window appears.

6 To set up your backup, click **Set up backup**.

*Note: If you are not using an administrator account, the User Account Control dialog box appears. You must type an administrator password and then click **Yes** to be able to continue.*

Tip

How can I choose the files I want to back up?

If you want to specify exactly which files you want to back up, click **Let me choose** in step **9** below and then click **Next** to continue. Windows will display a list of items on your computer that you can back up. A check mark (☑) appears beside each item that Windows will back up. To add or remove a check mark, click the box (☐) beside an item. When you finish selecting the items you want to back up, click **Next** to continue.

Tip

How can I keep my backups safe?

You should place the device on which you store your backup, such as an external hard drive, USB flash drive, CD or DVD, in a safe, fireproof location away from your computer. Storing your backup device away from your computer helps to protect your information in the event of a fire or the theft of your computer.

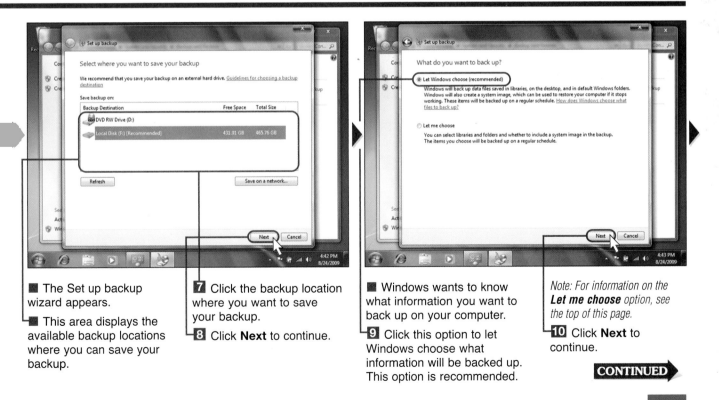

■ The Set up backup wizard appears.

■ This area displays the available backup locations where you can save your backup.

7 Click the backup location where you want to save your backup.

8 Click **Next** to continue.

■ Windows wants to know what information you want to back up on your computer.

9 Click this option to let Windows choose what information will be backed up. This option is recommended.

*Note: For information on the **Let me choose** option, see the top of this page.*

10 Click **Next** to continue.

CONTINUED

BACK UP YOUR FILES

If you let Windows choose what information will be backed up, Windows will back up the files in your Documents, Pictures, Music and Videos libraries as well as the files on your desktop.

If you have set up more than one user on your computer, Windows will back up the files belonging to every user.

BACK UP YOUR FILES (CONTINUED)

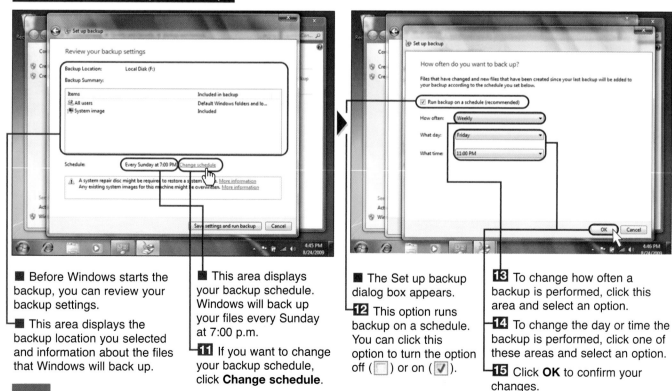

■ Before Windows starts the backup, you can review your backup settings.

■ This area displays the backup location you selected and information about the files that Windows will back up.

■ This area displays your backup schedule. Windows will back up your files every Sunday at 7:00 p.m.

11 If you want to change your backup schedule, click **Change schedule**.

■ The Set up backup dialog box appears.

12 This option runs backup on a schedule. You can click this option to turn the option off ( ) or on (✓).

13 To change how often a backup is performed, click this area and select an option.

14 To change the day or time the backup is performed, click one of these areas and select an option.

15 Click **OK** to confirm your changes.

Can I change my backup settings?

Yes. If you want to change the location where you will save your backup, the information you want to back up or the backup schedule, perform steps 1 to 5 on page 296 to open the Backup and Restore window. In the window, click **Change settings** and then perform steps 7 to 15 to change your settings. To save your changes, click **Save settings and exit**.

Note: If you are not using an administrator account, the User Account Control dialog box will appear. You must type an administrator password and then click **Yes** *to be able to continue.*

Can I perform a backup at any time?

Yes. You may not want to wait until your next scheduled backup to perform a backup. For example, you may want to immediately back up your files after you make important changes. To do so, perform steps 1 to 5 on page 296 to open the Backup and Restore window. In the window, click **Back up now** to immediately start the backup.

Note: If you are not using an administrator account, the User Account Control dialog box will appear. You must type an administrator password and then click **Yes** *to be able to continue.*

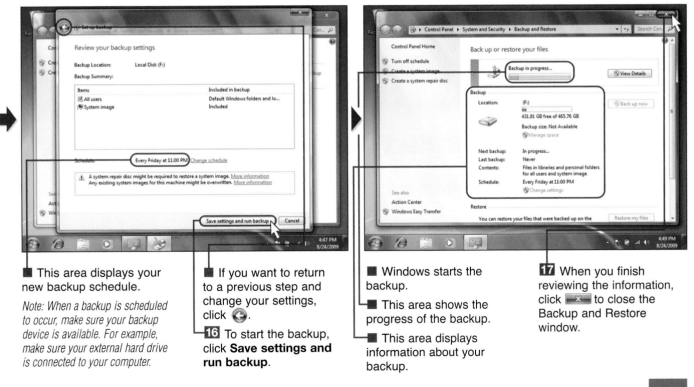

■ This area displays your new backup schedule.

Note: When a backup is scheduled to occur, make sure your backup device is available. For example, make sure your external hard drive is connected to your computer.

■ If you want to return to a previous step and change your settings, click ⬅.

16 To start the backup, click **Save settings and run backup**.

■ Windows starts the backup.

■ This area shows the progress of the backup.

■ This area displays information about your backup.

17 When you finish reviewing the information, click ✕ to close the Backup and Restore window.

RESTORE BACKED UP FILES

If files on your computer are lost, damaged or changed accidentally, you can use backup copies of the files to restore the files on your computer.

For information on backing up files on your computer, see page 296.

RESTORE BACKED UP FILES

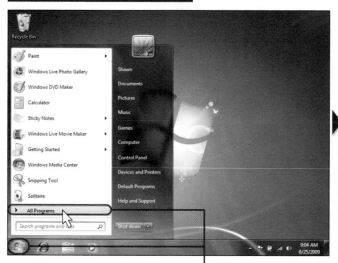

1 Connect the external hard drive that contains your backed up files to your computer.

■ If you backed up files to a USB flash drive, CD or DVD, connect the USB flash drive or insert the CD or DVD into your computer's drive.

Note: If the AutoPlay window appears, click [X] to close the window.

2 Click 🪟 to display the Start menu.

3 Click **All Programs**.

4 Click **Maintenance**.

5 Click **Backup and Restore**.

■ The Backup and Restore window appears.

6 Click **Restore my files** to restore files on your computer.

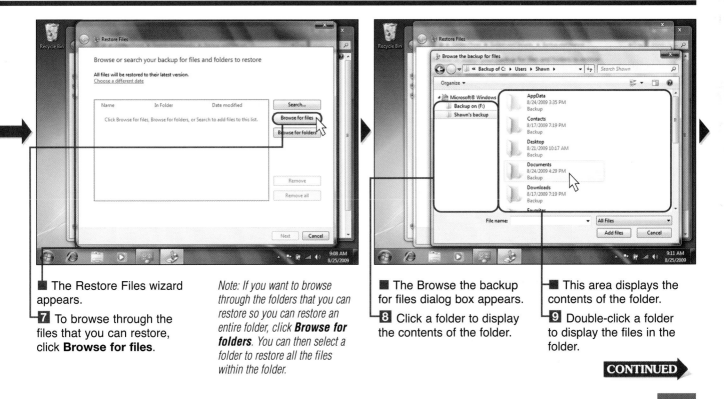

■ The Restore Files wizard appears.

7 To browse through the files that you can restore, click **Browse for files**.

*Note: If you want to browse through the folders that you can restore so you can restore an entire folder, click **Browse for folders**. You can then select a folder to restore all the files within the folder.*

■ The Browse the backup for files dialog box appears.

8 Click a folder to display the contents of the folder.

■ This area displays the contents of the folder.

9 Double-click a folder to display the files in the folder.

CONTINUED

RESTORE BACKED UP FILES

RESTORE TO: DESKTOP

When restoring files, you can choose the files you want to restore and the location where you want to place the restored files on your computer.

You may want to place the files you are restoring in a different location so that you do not accidentally overwrite any files that you want to keep.

RESTORE BACKED UP FILES (CONTINUED)

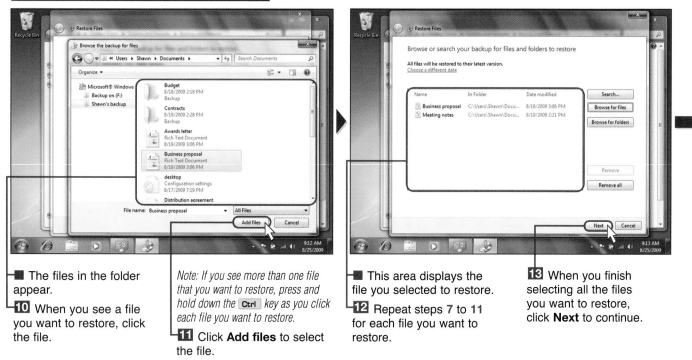

■ The files in the folder appear.

10 When you see a file you want to restore, click the file.

Note: If you see more than one file that you want to restore, press and hold down the **Ctrl** *key as you click each file you want to restore.*

11 Click **Add files** to select the file.

■ This area displays the file you selected to restore.

12 Repeat steps **7** to **11** for each file you want to restore.

13 When you finish selecting all the files you want to restore, click **Next** to continue.

Tip

When restoring my files, why does a dialog box appear?

When restoring files from a backup, if Windows comes across a file on your computer with the same name in the same location, a dialog box appears so you can choose what you want to do. Click the option you want.

Copy and Replace—replace the file on your computer with the backup file.

Don't copy—keep the file as is on your computer.

Copy, but keep both files—keep the file as is on your computer and place a renamed copy of the backup file on your computer.

 Tip

Can I restore my entire computer?

If Windows saved a system image during the backup, you can restore the contents of your computer if it stops working. A system image includes Windows as well as your computer settings, programs and files. Before performing a complete restoration of your computer, you should seek the advice and guidance of a computer professional.

Note: During a backup, a system image can only be saved on an external hard drive.

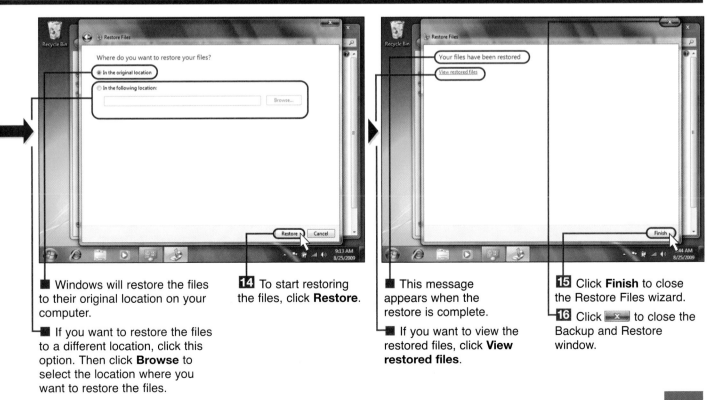

■ Windows will restore the files to their original location on your computer.

■ If you want to restore the files to a different location, click this option. Then click **Browse** to select the location where you want to restore the files.

14 To start restoring the files, click **Restore**.

■ This message appears when the restore is complete.

■ If you want to view the restored files, click **View restored files**.

15 Click **Finish** to close the Restore Files wizard.

16 Click ⬚✕⬚ to close the Backup and Restore window.

INDEX

INDEX

INDEX

INDEX

INDEX

INDEX

MARAN ILLUSTRATED™ Bartending
is the perfect book for those who want to
impress their guests with cocktails that are
both eye-catching and delicious. This indispensable guide explains everything
you need to know about bartending in
the most simple and easy-to-follow terms.
Maran Illustrated™ Bartending has recipes,
step-by-step instructions and over 400
full-color photographs of all the hottest mar-
tinis, shooters, blended drinks and warmers.
This guide also includes a
section on wine, beer and alcohol-free cocktails as well as information on all
of the tools, liquor and other supplies
you will need to start creating drinks
right away!

ISBN: 1-59200-944-1
Price: $19.99 US; $26.95 CDN
Page count: 256

MARAN ILLUSTRATED™ Piano is
an information-packed resource for
people who want to learn to play
the piano, as well as current musicians looking to hone their skills.
Combining full-color photographs and
easy-to-follow instructions, this guide
covers everything from the basics
of piano playing to more advanced
techniques. Not only does MARAN
ILLUSTRATED™ Piano show you how
to read music, play scales and chords
and improvise while playing with
other musicians, it also provides
you with helpful information for purchasing and caring for your piano.

ISBN: 1-59200-864-X

Price: $24.99 US; $33.95 CDN

Page count: 304

MARAN ILLUSTRATED™ Dog Training
is an excellent guide for both current
dog owners and people considering
making a dog part of their family.
Using clear, step-by-step instructions
accompanied by over 400 full-color photographs, MARAN ILLUSTRATED™ Dog
Training is perfect for any visual learner
who prefers seeing what to do rather
than reading lengthy explanations.

Beginning with insights into popular
dog breeds and puppy development,
this book emphasizes positive training
methods to guide you through socializ-
ing, housetraining and teaching your dog
many commands. You will
also learn how to work with problem
behaviors, such as destructive chewing.

ISBN: 1-59200-858-5

Price: $19.99 US; $26.95 CDN

Page count: 256

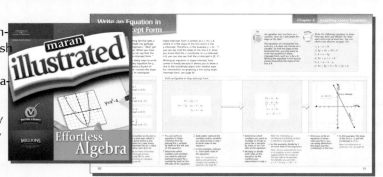

MARAN ILLUSTRATED™ Effortless Algebra

is an indispensable resource packed with crucial concepts and step-by-step instructions that make learning algebra simple. This guide is perfect for those who wish to gain a thorough understanding of algebra's concepts, from the most basic calculations to more complex operations.

Clear instructions thoroughly explain every topic and each concept is accompanied by helpful illustrations. This book provides all of the information you will need to fully grasp algebra. MARAN ILLUSTRATED™ Effortless Algebra also provides an abundance of practice examples and tests to put your knowledge into practice.

ISBN: 1-59200-942-5
Price: $24.99 US; $33.95 CDN
Page count: 304

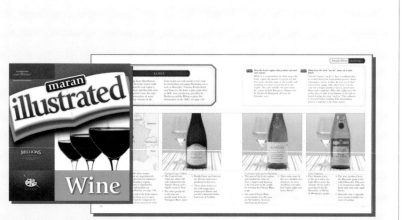

MARAN ILLUSTRATED™ Wine is an

indispensable guide for your journey into the world of wine. The information-packed resource is ideal for people who are just beginning to explore wine as well as for wine enthusiasts who want to expand their knowledge.

This full-color guide, containing hundreds of photographs, walks you step by step through tasting and serving wine, reading a wine label and creating a wine collection. You will also find in-depth information about the wines of the world. MARAN ILLUSTRATED™ Wine will also introduce you to sparkling wines and Champagne as well as fortified and sweet wines. You will learn the basics of how wine is made, how to pair the right wine with your meal and much more.

ISBN: 1-59863-318-X
Price: $24.99 US; $33.95 CDN
Page count: 288